Becoming SHEROES

STORIES OF HEARTSTRONG WOMEN

Dear Nelz,
Thank you so much
for helping with my dad's book!
So glad to have you.
Kaen

FILIPINA SHEROES

Performance Publishing
McKinney, TX

ISBN: 978-1-961781-05-4

Contents

Acknowledgement

Thank you to the Filipina Sheroes - each of you have been an inspiration to me not just through your stories, but through your own lives and personal endeavors.

Thank you to Gloria Sicam, Franki Ramirez, and April Agregado for your invaluable consultation, creative ideas, and overall support of this project and more.

My eternal appreciation to my mother, Cris Victoria, who has always been a source of strength and inspiration. There will never be enough words in this language or any other language that could express my love and gratitude for you. I am a strong woman because I was raised by one.

In March of 2022, The Lady Leaders Club launched their book Together We Rise as response to their need for their mutual support during the physical and often times emotional isolating time of Covid. These women leaders in the staffing industry had decided that writing a book together could both help them survive this challenging time emotionally as well as inspire others with their stories. Each woman's story talked about their own challenges and how they overcame them to become a stronger leader, mother, and role model.

During their launch event in Austin, I listened to them speak briefly about their story and flipped through the book, Together We Rise. I thought to myself, we have so many strong and inspiring Filipinas that have their own unique story of challenge and victory. We have many Filipinas who can share their life's story to help uplift others everywhere.

Six months later, at a conference in Las Vegas, I sought guidance from an author of Together We Rise , Leslie Vickery. Her encouragement and bold declaration during her talk—"There is a woman here who will write a similar book!"—lit a fire within me. Now, I really have to do this! I was committed now that it had been said out loud and now responsible to make this happen! It was the push I needed. The support and anticipation from those who approached me solidified my commitment.

If you say your vision and goal out loud, you become accountable and committed to them. The idea of writing a book was an idea for a long time until someone said it out loud in front of 300 women. I suddenly was accountable to these women to make it happen.

Back in Manila, I rallied my network and found 14 other women with stories of their own. All of them didn't feel that they were particularly extraordinary or that their story was particularly inspiring. However, I convinced them that we all have our own challenges, heartbreak, experiences, and personal endeavors that can be inspirational. They are heroes in their own right and to others around them. While we may believe that we are just living our lives or we are who we are, we all have a narrative that can spark a feeling, can ignite hope, and can push someone to action. Say it out loud.

The title Becoming Sheroes is reflective of the authors' evolution and growth from their experiences and challenges to become heroes of their own stories. It encompasses a journey of transformation molding them into protagonists of their own narratives – sheroes navigating life's complexities.

The title indicates an ongoing "becoming" as we continue to live, grow, and evolve. It is an ongoing journey rather than a final destination. Each chapter of our lives contributes to this ongoing narrative, promoting resilience and fortitude.

Our "becoming" is also influenced by how we uplift, inspire, and empower others. As we extend support, share our wisdom, and stand as examples of strong women, we not only shape our narratives, but also influence and empower those around us. This mutual exchange of empowerment contributes to collective strength. Empowered women empower women as they say. We become "heart strong" with each challenge and experience and each giving back to others. This idea of "heart strong" embodies resilience grown through challenges and experiences, emotional bravery gained from adversity. Each obstacle overcome, each act of giving back, contributes to this receptacle of strength empowering us to face future challenges with courage and compassion.

In honor of my mother and maternal grandmother, I founded the Victoria Heartstrong Organization, a non-profit dedicated to aiding high school and college girls from underprivileged backgrounds. Our primary goal is to provide comprehensive support for these young women's education, spanning financial assistance and a range of enriching programs. Proceeds generated from Becoming Sheroes will directly fund these invaluable initiatives.

Embarking on this book project alongside these remarkable women and others has been a "becoming" of my own. It's been about conquering my inner doubts, embracing a project poised for substantial impact, and dedicating myself to a lifelong mission of empowering others. Amidst this, I've cultivated friendships with these inspiring women. It's been a lesson that becoming a shero is a continuous journey with many stories that may not always end in success, but will always lead to discovery.

Monica Maralit

Marissa Atienza

Sheroes: A Journey of Healing, Empowerment, and Motherhood

Introduction

Embarking on the remarkable journey of motherhood has been a tapestry woven with vivid moments of joy, complex challenges, and profound self-discovery. Within its intricate threads lie stories of triumph, struggle, and the transformative power of embracing vulnerability and empowerment. Here's a recount of my personal voyage as a single mother: exploring the highs and lows that have sculpted my path and the invaluable lessons I've learned along the way.

Chapter 1: Juno's Embrace

Me: Baby, this job is not good for my mental health. I want to quit. Do you want to go back to Cebu, or do you prefer to live here in Manila?

Juno: I just want you to be happy, Mama.

I bawled my eyes out that night.

His words, "I just want you to be happy, Mama," pierced through my heart. In that tender moment, I realized the depth of our bond and the unwavering support he offers. This was just one chapter in our story, a testament to the love that has sustained us through thick and thin. Juno has constantly been a steadfast presence in my life - an anchor in tumultuous seas.

Juno saw me through my highest and lowest times. I am always thankful that I am privileged to be both a mother and a woman on my own terms despite the challenges of single motherhood. I always say that in his own ways, Juno allowed me to grow in my own time – heal my wounds, fall in love again, and follow my dreams.

Chapter 2: Confronting My Demons

Life is an unpredictable journey, and sometimes its twists and turns can lead us to the darkest of places. The aftershocks of grieving from deaths, failed relationships, and emotional instability hit me hard in 2018. I found myself wrestling with anger management issues and struggling to contain the storm within. The journey towards healing, a formidable path that ultimately led to my transformation, demanded that I confront my inner demons.

> **Juno saw me through my highest and lowest times. I am always thankful that I am privileged to be both a mother and a woman on my own terms despite the challenges of single motherhood. I always say that in his own ways, Juno allowed me to grow in my own time – heal my wounds, fall in love again, and follow my dreams.**

The scene in my head is still clear. I was being too violent, throwing whatever my hand touched. I was sobbing and screaming incoherently. My relatives pulled Juno out of the room and locked me inside.

In that moment, deafening voices and horrifying thoughts of self-destruction seemed to pull me into a black hole, making me defenseless against my overwhelming emotions. Words and critiques about me being too emotional kept on playing in my head, trapping me in a void, replaying past mistakes and failures.

These episodes happened several times, and Juno had to witness one or two. They became even more frequent when Juno had to be taken away to the islands.

Chapter 3: A Pivotal Decision

This wasn't the first time that Juno had to be taken away from me.

Years earlier, I faced a heart-wrenching decision: sending Juno to live with relatives in the province while I worked in the city. At a young age, Juno's eyes were opened to the reality of life – some relationships are bound to fail, that money doesn't come easy, that Papa has gone somewhere else, and that Mama needed to work. I wished Juno didn't have to see what a failed marriage looks like at the age of two, but I'm a believer that things had to happen and that every event had a purpose. While the marriage breakdown was agonizing, it marked a turning point in my life. It became a period of self-renewal and rebuilding as I embarked on a mission to re-establish myself and heal from past wounds.

Chapter 4: Reunion and Rediscovery

The following year, I took Juno back from the province. I felt so relieved to have him back home again. Juno's return to my life ignited a newfound sense of purpose and resilience within me. Navigating single parenthood was no small feat, but together we braved its challenges, forged unforgettable memories, and shared cherished moments.

I remember Juno having this homework wherein he had to answer "What does your mom do?" What he wrote was, *"Nothing, she just sleeps all day. But she's brainy. She knows a lot."* Though brainy sounded nice, the first sentence somehow pinched my heart. I never forgot about it; his statement lingered for years.

Moments like these made me question my value as a mother. No matter how many times I validated the need to provide, it was always heartbreaking for me to step out of the house with a child in tears begging me not to leave for work. I can't imagine how much more the pain is for parents working overseas.

This went on for years until that one fateful anger management episode. Along with some unexpected and critical life events, my son had to move back again to the islands. It might have been an unpopular decision for others, but as a parent, I knew that move was best at that time. And so, again, I chose to be left all alone in Manila to work.

To say that my whole world shattered is an understatement. Not seeing my son for months led to even more episodes of mental breakdown as the question "What kind of mother am I?" gnawed at my insides. The guilt engulfed me.

I had to endure these episodes alone at home with only my pets to comfort me. During those times, my garage was filled with cigarette butts and bottles of beers and wine. I battled through those voices and black holes on my own, praying that I would still be granted another day to wake up.

Until one night, I had another episode while at work.

Chapter 5: A Hovering Storm Cloud

In the middle of my shift, I was rushed to the ER. I remember treading along the streets of Commonwealth at midnight, just as the clock ticked to May 1. It was a vivid memory that the sound of the ambulance siren automatically plays in my head when I recall that scene. What a way to spend Labor Day!

I had myself checked up years ago regarding this, and the doctor plainly told me to "avoid extreme emotions." I've always found it to be almost impossible, especially for an empath like me. It sounded like a non-threatening problem back then, but that ER incident was indeed a wake-up call. I knew I had to do something.

This piqued my journey in life coaching.

Chapter 6: Saved by a Purr

I went on with my life that year, learning to live away from Juno and dealing with my emotional instability. I was still traveling and performing well at work. I was still drinking away at parties and smoking my lungs out.

The final straw happened while I was on a two-month business trip in Cebu.

It was almost 3:00 a.m. While the guests in the hotel were fast asleep in their rooms, there I was carried by my friend as I went home drunk... again.

I can still recount everything that happened that day. From a night of hard partying, I woke up to a number of bruises, a throbbing headache, and a broken wristwatch. I laughed at myself for I couldn't remember anything, but my musing was halted when a chat message popped on my phone.

"*Ate*, Duchess is dead."

I was in total shock. I felt the Earth had stopped moving for what felt like hours.

Duchess was a Siamese cat that I adopted in October 2016. She rolled her eyes at me when we first met but purred right away when I carried her. She was my first cat, and hers is the first purr I've ever received. Right then and there, I knew she must be aptly named, Duchess. She was a playful yet moody cat. She loved going out, tendering me worried sick for days. But she never missed greeting me when I came home ... that is if she was home. She was elegant like royalty, yet doting like a puppy. Many times, I thought we were similar in so many ways and that my level of stubbornness had finally met a match.

She was my constant companion at home, especially during that time when my family members had to move to the islands to take care of my ill *Lolo*. She was my watchman, my confidante, and my avid listener. She was only four months old when I took her in in 2016, and then she passed on in 2018. And it all happened when I was away for that two-month work trip.

Days before Duchess passed, I had another episode in Cebu. But at that time, Duchess wasn't around to watch me wail. I remember screaming in my hotel room cursing myself, cursing everyone, thinking of ways to stop feeling hurt, but at the same time praying that God would forgive me and wake me up in the morning. It was a hard phase to go through, and it is something definitely difficult to explain, especially to those who haven't experienced it themselves. But the demons in my head, at that time, were real. And no matter how much of a logical person I am who wants science to explain everything, I heard them. And they told me to stop existing.

Duchess was there with me during the same episodes in Manila. Maybe she heard the voices too, maybe not. But she was always generous in allowing her fur to be soaked in tears. My fellow feline parents and friends said that maybe Duchess missed me so much and died of depression. Maybe she thought I wasn't coming back home. My cousins said she wasn't eating much since I had left, until they found her cold and motionless that morning. But for me, I felt like Duchess gave up herself to save me.

My beloved cat became a silent witness to my struggles and triumphs. Her soothing presence provided solace during my darkest hours. In her, I found a kindred spirit – one who offered unconditional love and comfort. Duchess's passing left an indelible mark, serving as a catalyst for my metamorphosis and a poignant reminder of the power of connections.

Chapter 7: A Revelation of Strength

Duchess's departure marked a turning point in my life, propelling me towards a path of healing and empowerment. No longer willing to succumb to my inner turmoil, I embarked on a transformative journey, shedding my past and embracing a future defined by resilience and strength. The shackles of self-destruction gave way to a newfound appreciation for life's preciousness.

All of these moments in my life gave me the courage to let go of everything – my 30+ years life in Manila, my event management business, all my childhood memories and mementos, my career, and all the things that (I thought) defined me … everything for that one moment to be with my son again. During that time, I fervently prayed and asked Him to place me somewhere I could serve Him more.

True enough, God's grace is more powerful than all our wants and desires combined. My granted application to be relocated to Cebu was a testimony of God's love and mercy.

Ever since I moved to the island city, I've been able to spend more time with Juno. Frequent trips to the beach have been a regular adventure. Every time we board a boat or ship, we shriek "We are Voyagers!" like Moana did when she discovered her ancestors' hidden vintas in a cave. I talked to him about that homework one lazy afternoon under our mango tree and asked him again, "What do you think Mama does? What do you think of me?" This is what he said:

"Mama is a writer and a diver (scuba). Mama is lovable, sporty, beautiful ... and brainy."

Funny how he added brainy as an after-thought, as if he recalled his answer way back. His innocent understanding of what I do, his perception of me as "lovable, sporty, beautiful and brainy" warmed my heart and rekindled my determination to be the best version of myself. I felt grateful that in some way, he finally knew me. Although writing and diving were not really my profession (but side shticks), those two answers were a huge improvement from "Nothing." I love that he had "lovable" as the first on his list; for me, the other adjectives are cherries on top.

As they say, our children grow so fast, and before we know it, they are out there more with their friends than with us. This reminded me that I should be spending time with Juno as much as I could. I know this is a challenge for working single moms like me, but I believe that we can find ways to spend more quality time with our children before time runs out. I must admit that I've had a lot of opportunities while we were living together in the city, but cliché as it may sound, it is indeed never too late to start all over again.

If there's anything that Covid taught me, it's the privilege I have to spend more time with Juno and make up for the lost time.

The pandemic also gave birth to our life coaching start-up: Make Space PH.

Chapter 8: Harnessing Resilience Through Make Space PH

One day in 2018, I woke up, tearful and thankful, after battling an episode the night prior. Only God and Duchess knew how scary that breakdown looked and how hard I prayed that God would still wake me up. I'm blessed that He did and always does.

Three years later, I had my first ever paid speaking engagement series outside my workplace. To be invited as an external guest speaker is such an honor, and to do it professionally is a blessing. During this time, my best friend and I started offering 1:1 life coaching and doing livecasts on Facebook as Make Space PH.

Make Space PH started out as a passion project with my best friend, Virn, and with other people in our community who share the same advocacy. We believe that art heals and transforms pain into a masterpiece; therefore, we aspire to empower lives through transformative art and compassionate guidance. At Make Space PH, we are a collective of dedicated life coaches, psychologists, and mental health advocates whose mission is to empower individuals to embrace their inner resilience, navigate life's challenges, and unlock their true potential.

This opportunity to empower people with stories gave me another purpose. I know in my heart I was given another shot at life to inspire, empower, and help a soul or two to see life in a different light, especially when hope seemed bleak during the pandemic.

This opportunity to empower people with stories gave me another purpose. I know in my heart I was given another shot at life to inspire, empower, and help a soul or two to see life in a different light, especially when hope seemed bleak during the pandemic.

Chapter 9: Embracing Vulnerability

Through Make Space PH, I discovered the empowering nature of vulnerability. Sharing my story, struggles, and triumphs created a space for connection and healing. It is through vulnerability that we find our truest selves and cultivate meaningful connections with others. As I witnessed the transformation of those who crossed our path, I realized the profound impact of our willingness to open our hearts. As I looked back, those turning points and moments of solitude helped me know myself better. I learned that my true passion lies in finding my voice and in helping others find theirs.

Turning my so-called weakness into my strength, I was able to tap into another person's ability to re-acquaint with their inner selves and give them that space to be vulnerable. For me, that's my superpower. As one of my mentors used to say, "Mars, you are more than your emotional baggage."

The trials I faced cultivated an unwavering resilience within me. Each challenge became an opportunity for growth, strengthening my resolve and shaping my identity. I learned that my emotions, once perceived as a weakness, were in fact beautiful pieces of me that contributed to my unique story and that made me, ME.

Chapter 10: A Mother's Legacy

As I reflect on my journey, I am reminded of the legacy I wish to leave for Juno. My transformation from despair to empowerment serves as a guiding light, inspiring him to embrace his own path with authenticity and resilience. Through my experiences, I hope to instill in him the importance of navigating life's challenges with grace and determination.

This reminded me of another conversation I had with him.

Me: Baby, should I continue doing what I do – writing, coaching? I'm just so tired.

Juno: Don't. Someone might need you. You might inspire someone.

And that's what I aim to do moving forward – make spaces for people to find their own voices and inspire others to find theirs.

Conclusion: An Ongoing Odyssey

As my journey continues, I am fueled by the knowledge that embracing vulnerability and empowerment has the power to transform lives. The impact of Make Space PH, the stories of those we've touched, and the realization that every day is an opportunity for growth reaffirm my commitment to this path. As I navigate the chapters yet to be written, I invite you to embark on your own journey of self-discovery, resilience, and empowerment – no matter how arduous – guided by the power of vulnerability and the hope for a kinder tomorrow.

This chapter provides a glimpse into my ongoing voyage, highlighting the ever-evolving nature of my path. Along with Make Space PH, I flourish, touching the lives of many. My commitment to empowerment remains steadfast.

As I always say: *Let's keep learning and keep loving more.*

Marissa Atienza

Marissa Atienza is a certified life coach, trainer, and co-founder of Make Space PH, a life coaching and consultancy startup. She has over 10 years of experience in creating and delivering powerful programs that spark positive change and growth in people's lives.

As a keynote speaker and facilitator, she covers topics such as Personal Development, Emotional Intelligence, Mental Wellness, and DEI (Diversity, Equity, and Inclusion). She is also a highly accomplished Learning and Development Professional with expertise in coaching, learning design and evaluation, project management, and communication strategy. She has led and contributed to numerous initiatives that enhanced performance, fostered a culture of learning, and promoted diversity and inclusion within various organizations. She has received multiple awards and recognition for her work and impact in the field of learning and development.

Marissa is a passionate storyteller who encourages and empowers people to find their voice. As an arts and culture enthusiast, she aspires to specialize in culture research and roam around the world. She can talk and interact for hours but can get very serious in getting quiet time with her wine and thoughts. On most occasions, she goes off with her son, Juno, as they fight for justice with her lasso of truth.

Linkedin: https://www.linkedin.com/in/marissa-atienza-47316711b/
Facebook: https://www.facebook.com/missmars.lifecoach

Karen Batungbacal

JUMP IN WITH BOTH FEET, ALWAYS

Never in a million years would my younger self have imagined where I am now and who I have become. My life may not have been all good with the inevitable heartaches and mistakes, but it has mostly been great.

I confess, I am still a highly functioning contradictory mess. After 30 years of achievement, I struggle with "imposter syndrome." I feel massive guilt about not being the best mother, wife, daughter, sister, or friend.

For a long time, I've always felt stretched too thin and caught in the familial role as the '*taga-salo*' (catcher) of family, friends, the company – whatever. The '*taga-salo*' focuses on keeping the peace within the family and needs control while staying emotionally distant. Psychologist Dr. Honey Carandang explains that most of the '*taga-salo*'s' self-concept relies on how she can please others in her group.

But now I finally know and accept who I am and who I have become – and I am happy.

I think my story is one of guilt, having been born into privilege, and wondering whether I belong. I vividly remember two incidents when I was about ten years old. One was when we walked down the side stairwell of the Cultural Center of the Philippines to quickly exit from a ballet. I was shocked to see this dirty young boy sleeping on newspapers in the dark. My father shouted in surprise, and the fear in that young boy's eyes still haunts me.

The other incident was when a group of young beggars plastered their faces onto the window of our car. Those eyes continue to torment me.

This fear of destitution and desire to belong may be why I strive hard and feel strongly about giving back.

In 2020, during the pandemic, my son and I cooked and handed out meals to street children along Roxas Boulevard. It was heart-breaking.

One of the joys of hiring thousands of newbies into the BPO companies I ran was speaking to them during induction. I would remind them that while they were joining the prestigious multinationals I was running, most Filipinos don't have the same opportunities, so it's our responsibility to give back. I encouraged my team to volunteer with me, whether for Gawad Kalinga, Mind Museum, Hands-On Manila, or CNN Hero of the Year Efren Peñaflorida. We volunteer because it's by the grace of God that we are where we are.

Early years

I am the middle child of three girls. My sisters took after our mother, a tall, beautiful *mestiza* (fair-skinned woman). I was the *morena* (darker skinned woman) or *kayumanggi* (brown) one, the Batungbacal daughter. Sunblock wasn't a thing in the '60s and '70s, and since I loved to play outdoors, I was very dark. I didn't burn and peel like my sisters and my *mestiza* maternal cousins. My sisters remember a friend of my mother asking who I was: "*Quien es?*" and how surprised she was when my mother replied that I was one of her kids. Kids can be cruel, and my sisters and cousins loved to say I was adopted.

Even as a child, I was gregarious. I wanted to be noticed and stand out, so I was friendly and popular with my classmates. By sixth grade, I developed an interest in academics and excelled.

I also felt a bit guilty that I wasn't the boy. Since our eldest was female, I felt like I should've been the son my dad wanted. Maybe that's why I took up engineering, loved cars, and did "boyish" things.

My paternal grandparents were educated middle-class, managers in the Postal Service. My grandmother was the first Filipina teletype operator. My father went to public school in Santa Ana, Manila. He was brilliant, a University of the Philippines scholar from high school through college and medical school. He was in Upsilon and was so ambitious that he got a scholarship to Harvard Medical School for his ophthalmology studies.

My mother was born into more class but not wealth, Ilonggos from Iloilo and Bacolod. My grandfather worked for the Elizaldes and managed to buy a sugar hacienda in Negros. They socialized quite well with the Ilonggo elite. At age seven, my mother was sent to be an *interna* (stay-in student) at St. Scholastica's College Manila along with her sister. She became a scholar at Maryknoll College before leaving to pursue studies in Madrid.

With this background, my sisters and I were expected to achieve scholastically, and we all did. But I think that as a middle child (who wasn't the cutest one), I felt I had to accomplish in other ways too.

Complicated career choices

My journey was not linear. I wanted to be a lawyer, but my mom nixed it, saying lawyers were plentiful and that I was too emotional. She enrolled me in chemistry since my math and science grades were high.

I shifted to chemical engineering, dreaming I'd be one of those payload specialists working at the National Aeronautics and Space Administration (NASA). I needed a doctorate for this, so I got a scholarship to Princeton, only to find out much later that solitary research work in a dungeon-like laboratory wasn't for extroverted me.

Pursuing chemical engineering wasn't a mistake. It disciplined my mind and sharpened my analytical abilities. And somehow, it made people think I was so intelligent, getting a Princeton scholarship. After almost three years at Princeton, I left. That was the first shift in my career.

Then I learned that several chief executive officers (CEOs) in manufacturing were chemical engineers. I wanted to be on the business side, but my credentials thus far weren't cut out for it. I didn't want to work in a plant, yet when I applied to Coca-Cola, Mobil Oil, Proctor & Gamble, and Pfizer, they all put me in research.

One of my professors at Princeton advised me to look for management training programs to get into management. I got one with American President Lines (APL). I knew nothing about shipping and logistics, but I knew that APL would teach me.

I was trained at their fancy Wall Street office but worked at the railyards, trains, and ports to board container vessels. It was FUN. I eventually rose through the ranks and became logistics head in another male-dominated space.

I loved working in logistics. When I was 27, I was stationed in Manila for two years to help set up APL's customer service operation for the Philippines and Guam. Little did I know the impact this supposed short-term assignment would later play on where my career would go.

Also, I met a man who would be my first husband. After a whirlwind three-week courtship, we got married.

Marry in haste, repent at leisure. Our marriage ended after four years and two kids. I had to soldier on. No one at any company I worked for, APL then Citibank, knew what I was going through at home. Still, I don't think getting married was a mistake because it produced my two eldest children and gave me a wonderful family of in-laws and a good co-parent. However, I will always regret raising them as a single mom.

At this point, with zero banking background, I joined Citibank. It's a great company, but I learned that the rigid structure inherent in a bank was not for me. It also drove me crazy when customers would argue with account managers over petty things. And it didn't make me feel good that my job was to make the super-wealthy even wealthier.

Fortune favors the bold.

I am competitive, a hard worker, and a people pleaser. I want to win, but I won't ride roughshod over anyone. I do not like confrontational situations and shy away from them. Thank goodness these encounters have been few and far between.

My competitive nature and work ethic made me visible to my superiors and gave me access to opportunities. These qualities prepared me for when luck would come.

I received a call from the Lopez group to help start a new telecommunications company to go head-to-head with PLDT (formerly the Philippine Long Distance Telephone Company). Once more, I didn't know anything about the telecom industry, but I jumped in.

My biggest 'aha!' moment came in 1999. I read about the business process outsourcing (BPO) work America Online (AOL) was doing in Clark, Pampanga. Why can't we do the work here? I was already handling customer service for Bayantel, Meralco, Maynilad, and Skycable. It set me on the trajectory to become a pioneer in this industry I love.

In 2000, I started the first Philippine-owned call center, C-Cubed, backed by the Lopez Group. It set the tone for the rest of my career, over 20 years in BPO.

The BPO industry brings much-needed employment and so much opportunity. For this, I gained the moniker "mother" of the Philippine BPO industry, but I am not sure I deserve this.

Another 'aha!' moment was when I was with JPMorgan Chase (JPMC) from 2009 to 2012. Part of my job was to create employee groups like PRIDE for the LGBTQIA+ and Women's Interactive Network (WIN).

At first, I thought setting up WIN in Manila wasn't necessary; after all, I was a woman running JPMC. The Philippine president then, Gloria Macapagal-Arroyo, was a woman. I didn't think it was relevant until we held the first meeting.

A young vice president asked us how to convince her husband and in-laws that she wanted a banking career. She didn't want to be a stay-at-home mom. Hearing that shocked me, and I realized that my upbringing isn't traditionally Filipino but very Western and privileged. No one ever stopped me from working.

While I was sensitive to PRIDE and LGBTQIA+, I wasn't with my gender. It was a big reminder that most Filipinos aren't raised like the prosperous ones in Metro Manila.

I am also so proud of the young women managers I hired way back in 1995 to help me start the customer services group of Bayantel. The first one, Bettina Salmo, is now the Philippine Country Head and Managing Director of JP Morgan Chase & Co.'s Business Center in the Philippines with over 16,000 staff, the same position I held a decade ago. Joy Padlan heads the Philippine Shared Services at Sagility with over 13,000 people, and Raquel Capinpin is the Global Operations and Client Services Site Lead for the Philippines of DTCC. They were all in their late twenties to early thirties when they joined me in 1995 and when we created C-Cubed a scant five years later and I am so thrilled to see they are all leaders in the BPO industry.

Letting go and letting God

These days, I am much calmer. I accept that I can't control everything. My faith is much stronger because I work on it.

At this stage of my life, my most important assets are my family and friends. My second husband, with his total acceptance of life and all its challenges, is my rock. He brings comic relief as we constantly make each other laugh. My kids, now adults, have become my teachers. Their unique experiences and views on life expanded mine.

It sounds cliché, but the fear of poverty (like those poor kids I saw growing up) and wanting to belong drove me to become what some would call a workaholic.

I don't need to be the chief of anything now. The passing of my parents reminded me that I must give the same time and attention to my interior and spiritual growth and the relationships I value in my life.

Below is what I've learned about inspiring leadership—both as a businessperson and a woman—and how you can put it into practice.

Be authentic.

Since JPMC, I had a few more career moves. Once, I left an excellent job for a lot more money. I knew the CEO from the U.S. was not the nicest, but the money beckoned. In less than two years, the company and I parted ways as we didn't have the same values. I realized that money isn't everything; in choosing your life partner or your place of employment, you must share common values.

I learned the importance of being yourself. Don't suppress your personality just because you are at work. As Facebook Chief Operating Officer Sheryl Sandberg said, "Presenting leadership as a list of carefully defined qualities, like being strategic, analytical, and performance-oriented, no longer holds. True leadership stems from individuality that is honestly and sometimes imperfectly expressed. Leaders should strive for authenticity over perfection."

Don't be afraid to make mistakes.

Good leaders know that they don't know everything. They understand that learning is a constant and ongoing process. Take it from former IBM CEO Ginni Rometty: "I learned to always take on things I'd never done before. Growth and comfort do not coexist."

> **So, step out of your comfort zone. You won't always have all the answers or all the data. You may have a sense or a vision of what you want to do, but we are not in control of our destiny, so expect yourself to be making mistakes.**

So, step out of your comfort zone. You won't always have all the answers or all the data. You may have a sense or a vision of what you want to do, but we are not in control of our destiny, so expect yourself to be making mistakes.

It was a risk for me to leave engineering, but it helped pave the way for my eventual career in BPO. I took several leaps of faith in my career, and this *lakas ng loob* (courage) has served me well.

Be bold; trust your instincts and intuition because there is absolutely nothing that you can't bounce back from. And don't forget that a sense of humor will see you through anything.

EMBRACE YOUR FEMININE SIDE.

All of us have both masculine and feminine characteristics. It's feminine to be collaborative and empathetic, to think more about how people feel. That's critically important for leaders today. If you don't reach the hearts of your employees, they won't invest in your company, your customers, or your vision.

As Maya Angelou said, "I've learned that people will forget what you said, people will forget what you did, but people will never forget how you made them feel."

Come to think of it, "the Female" and "the Filipino" are more relationship-focused than results-oriented. Both value harmony, consensus, and how people feel. They like to vent and speak and are more inclusive in decision-making. Both are detail-oriented, allowing for excellent planning and execution.

It's also a feminine trait to be intuitive, internally and socially. You won't always have complete information when making decisions. Usually, your gut feeling about things will be spot-on, so treasure that intuition as much as analysis and logic. The educational system can tend to beat it out of you; hang on to it. Your intuition is what will help you take leaps of faith.

Take time to renew and recharge.

Carve out time to work on yourself. Too many people have managed to convince themselves they can't change. Don't let that happen to you.

Invest in yourself. Renew your sense of purpose, restore your enthusiasm, and value your me-time. Work on YOU - physically, intellectually, and spiritually. Look out for yourself, as you are your number one project.

> **Invest in yourself. Renew your sense of purpose, restore your enthusiasm, and value your me-time. Work on YOU - physically, intellectually, and spiritually. Look out for yourself, as you are your number one project.**

Each of us is a finite resource, so take the time to rejuvenate and replenish your well. You need it to function for yourself and those you love and work with.

So, please make the time in your calendars for your "me time" and "development time."

Be prepared to listen.

My golden rule of management is I manage how I want to be managed. Early in my career, I understood the power of the team. I learned to be collaborative and consultative, to listen, and surrender control.

Leadership is about enabling people. They are your best resource, so listen to their feedback and encourage their dreams. That's the first step in building high-performing teams.

Marillyn Hewson, the former CEO of Lockheed Martin, once said, "Good leaders organize and align people around what the team needs to do. Great leaders motivate and inspire people with WHY they're doing it. That's purpose. And that's the key to achieving something truly transformational."

Find people you trust.

As I pivoted from engineering to logistics, banking, and telecommunications, I dared to take on these challenges because people believed in me.

Similarly, seek advisors and people who inspire you. Mentors and a community of elders you respect will counsel and push you. Let them stretch you. They see you in a different light, so trust in their vision and take on the challenges they give you. As Educational Equity Champion Cosette Gutierrez said, "If your mentors only tell you that you are awesome, it's time to find other mentors."

Also, treasure your support system. We all need life mentors. Aside from your family, build multiple communities and select these as best you can as you will share your journey with them.

What was so helpful and nourishing for me were the classmates I grew up with, from kindergarten to high school, those who were with me from my ugly duckling phase to my annulment to my remarriage.

My friends include the amazing leaders at the Filipina CEO Circle. There were only 20 of us at first; now there are over 70. Many of us had imposter syndrome, too; even if we had reached the top of our companies, we would feel it was for other reasons.

Create a similar sisterhood that will see you through your biggest challenges. They will tell you the truth.

Commit to commit.

The key themes in my life so far have been hard work, flexibility, courage, and resilience.

You may struggle to find a good work/life balance, but you can commit to certain things. Make some things sacred or immovable, and go from there.

If there's anything worth remembering from my story thus far, it's to love and accept yourself, warts and all. No one else will unless you do, so be kind to yourself and others. There are no shortcuts in life. Work hard and give everything your best shot. Be courageous and flexible. Nothing we do is permanent, even our mistakes, so don't sweat the small stuff.

As I write this, I'm 62 years old. I retired from corporate life two years ago. Life never stops throwing challenges, even as I enter another phase. I am also old enough to understand that I have to go with the flow since I know I'm not the sole decision-maker in my life. For me, as a practicing Catholic, it's God. For others, it may be the universe. I'm just glad to have made the right choices and look forward to my next adventure.

Karen V. Batungbacal

Karen is a recognized leader and strategic senior executive, who has built and managed small- to large-scale operations; from regional teams of 30 staff to over 10,000 in multiple industries across Asia Pacific and the U.S.

She is a chemical engineer by training but is best known as a pioneer in the Business Process Off-shoring and Shared Services space, having built and led companies in this sector since 2000, such as ICT Group, JP Morgan Chase, and Optum. She co-founded and was the first President of IT and Business Process Association of the Philippines, the BPO industry voice, where she is still a Senior Advisor to the Board. Similarly, with Global In-house Center Council, which she previously chaired. She is a member of the Filipina CEO Circle and a Governor of the Management Association of the Philippines. She is an Independent Director and a Fellow of the Institute of Corporate Directors.

Karen graduated Magna Cum Laude from the University of Notre Dame in Chemical Engineering and has a Master's in the same field from Princeton University.

She was named Outstanding Chemical Engineer 2010 by the Philippine Board of Chemical Engineering, and in 2014 and 2016, was twice awarded the 100 Most Influential Filipina Women in the World.

She is a happy wife to Joey De Venecia III, a mother of four, is devoted to her family, theatre, travel and food.

LinkedIn: linkedin.com/in/karen-batungbacal

Rebecca Bustamante

UNBREAKABLE

How does one deal with the cards that life hands you? Ask people who've gone through a lot, and they'll show you that it is hope and the sense of purpose that energizes them to rise from their challenging situations.

There is a reason why you are reading my words. I hope I can help you achieve your dreams with what I have learned from my own journey.

If you look up pictures of me online, you will probably see me smiling in my corporate clothes, speaking in front of groups or hanging out with impressive people. You're might think my story is about surviving the tough corporate world and overcoming men who didn't want me to succeed.

But it isn't. I found the corporate world welcoming to those who work hard and behave ethically. I certainly don't think of men as evil adversaries. I love the men in my life. They have mainly been supporters and friends who wanted the best for me.

I never in my wildest dreams thought I would be speaking in front of thousands of people in different countries or meeting with CEOs and Presidents. I consider myself just a little girl who worked hard, took risks, and followed her dreams.

My life isn't really the Cinderella story that many are inclined to believe. It was a 30-year transformation that took a lot of work and help from other people. It begins in Dasol, Pangasinan, where I was born and raised as the seventh child in a family of 11 children.

I grew up in a poverty-stricken environment. My family lived in what the UN called abject poverty – less than Php50 ($1) per day. Our nipa hut had no electricity, no water, and the toilet was often just the backyard. As a child, I had sores on my arms and legs that never healed, leaving round scars that never went away. My stomach was enlarged abnormally because of tape worm infestations and other reasons.

My parents had no steady income. I was keen to help feed the large family by selling bread and ice candy as a small child to buy rice. I sold fish and collected scrap wood in the afternoon with my siblings. We would sell whatever we found that someone might buy. Life could be unforgiving, but we kept our joy by staying together.

This was my start in life, but I am not at all bitter or upset by it. In life, it doesn't matter where you come from. What matters is where you are going.

Life was still a struggle. There were many people putting me down, looking down at my family for being so poor, and saying hurtful things about us. But I didn't let that stop me from continuing to work. They were not important. I was doing what I needed to do, which was to provide food for the family and send my siblings to school.

After finishing high school, I relocated to an industrial region called Bataan to work in a factory making gloves. With my small piece-work income, I made sure to send money back home to help my mother feed the family and send my sisters and brothers to school.

When I was 18 years old, my mother was diagnosed with lung cancer. I quit my job so I could help care for her. We were so poor that we could not afford the proper medical help that she needed. I remember how the doctor in our hospital would almost ignore us in the early days of my mother's prognosis because we didn't have any money to pay.

I was often the one making the tough decisions for my mother because my father and siblings were not able. I was frustrated because I saw my mother dying, and I wasn't able to provide for the care she needed. It broke my heart to see her lying in bed writhing with pain.

But for my mother's sake, I had to put up a brave front. My mother was scared of dying because of what would happen to her youngest children. It needed to be me who would commit to feed them and put them through school. I held my mother's hand tightly and told her, "Mommy, I'll do everything to look after them."

After that, she closed her eyes and passed away. I think she was waiting for me to say that so she could rest.

I vowed to fulfill my promise, even if I wasn't really the eldest but the seventh child—lucky number seven as I like to consider myself. I took the role of acting like the eldest by taking care of the household. Initially, I got odd jobs to make money and worked as a janitor at the tiny Rural Bank of Dasol. It was called a bank, but it was a very small business giving loans to poor people in the town.

I vowed to fulfill my promise, even if I wasn't really the eldest but the seventh child—lucky number seven as I like to consider myself. I took the role of acting like the eldest by taking care of the household.

It was then I discovered that our family house was about to be foreclosed on. My dad had put a mortgage on it and couldn't pay the money back. There was no other option for me but to find a better paying job to pay the mortgage or the family would have no place to live. The only way to make that kind of money was to work overseas.

Outside my Comfort Zone

At 19, I packed my little bag and left my small hometown to be a domestic helper in Singapore. I worked for a Singaporean family in their 3-bedroom flat. My boss was an aircraft technician with his wife and their two daughters.

Despite being shy and extremely naïve, I made sure to ask my boss to explain their expectations of me. I listened closely to what they said and resolved to do more than was expected of me. Like clockwork every day, I would clean, cook, buy the groceries, and watch over the young children.

The schedule was tough. I woke up at 5:00 a.m. every day to do the laundry, fix breakfast, and start cleaning. I didn't finish until around 11:00 p.m. when everyone went to sleep. I only had one day off per month (legal at the time). It was my first time away from home, and I was so lonely for my own family that I often cried by myself. I survived by thinking about the future.

I wanted to do a good job so my employer would like me, and hopefully then I could pursue my dream of getting a college degree. Because I grew up so poor, my goal was to help my siblings. I had graduated from high school but wanted to be more educated so I could accomplish more in life. I wanted to enroll in accounting courses at the Singapore Institute of Management so I could learn how money works. The problem was that I could not attend classes because I worked day and night. I was so fortunate to find a wonderful instructor who agreed to see me on my one day off each month. She gave me assignments on that one day, corrected them the next month, and gave me new ones for self-study.

From 11:00 p.m. to 1:00 a.m. most nights, when the family was asleep, I quietly studied in my tiny room. For three years, I slept a lot less than I should have. I learned many concepts that later helped me in my businesses. Even though it wasn't possible for me to graduate, it was worth it.

The Great White North

My plan was to work in Singapore for four years and then migrate to Canada where I could become a permanent resident and bring my brothers and sisters later. I focused on this dream and pursued it with determination and discipline.

I arrived in Canada in 1990. I worked with a family as a nanny, but I fancied myself as an "RN," a registered nanny. Again, I resolved to be the best nanny I could be for my new family. Working conditions were better in Canada. I worked only five days a week with a good family that became so dear to me.

Education remained a priority. In Toronto, I enrolled at Ryerson University's graduate courses in accounting and marketing. I also joined a direct-sales organization and sold kitchenware to my Filipino friends.

My schedule was to work all day and do a good job for my nice Canadian family. On Monday and Wednesday nights, I took classes. At all other times, I carried my heavy suitcases of pots and pans on buses all around to show them to whomever wanted to see them.

I discovered that I enjoyed selling and had clear goals. I learned as much as I could about sales by reading books and listening to mentors. My target was to sell $5,000 each week, and my sales commission was 35%. I was often earning $7,000 per month. That was a lot of money 30 years ago, and I was still working full-time as a live-in nanny. I couldn't believe it was possible. I was able to buy myself a sexy Volvo car – a second-hand one but it still looked good.

I was living my dream. Imagine, I felt I was a movie star driving my car around. But that was then. Today, I wouldn't advise spending so much money on a superficial display. Fancy cars depreciate, and your money disappears. Real investments build wealth.

It was time to update my goals. I gave myself two years to be a nanny. After that, I wanted to spread my wings for bigger challenges that would eventually lead to my ultimate dream of establishing my own business and being my own boss.

I upscaled my sales ability by joining the direct-selling beauty company, Mary Kay Cosmetics. During my stint, I won awards such as Top Rookie Sales Director for North America, Top 10 Unit Sales Award (Canada), and Top 10 Personal Sales Award (Canada). My highest post at the company was Senior Sales Director.

I always enjoyed talking to people and inspiring them, especially women. This brought me to deliver regular training presentations for large crowds of up to 500 participants in national company functions.

Land My Man

My brothers and sisters had finished school, and it was time for me to focus on building my own family. I didn't have a clue about dating because I had only worked in my life. So the first thing I did was read books about men and what to do.

I read books like "How to Marry the Man of your Choice" and others. I made my usual goals for the type of man I wanted and put timelines for when it was to happen. I wrote out all my "requirements" for a husband and posted it on my wall.

One day, my girlfriend called me about a guy she knew who she said met my "requirements." We tried to figure out a way for me to meet him in a casual way, but we couldn't figure out anything that made sense. Finally, I just called him up and asked him out.

I had started going to the gym to make myself as pretty as possible, and I was becoming financially secure. When I met Richard, I was confident to be with him. I actually paid for the first date and the second, and even the third. It wasn't because he didn't expect to pay, but I would put my money out fast before he could do anything. He said later that of all the women he had dated, not one had done that. He said it was something that set me apart because I became as asset in his mind rather than a liability. It also made him feel good that a woman wanted to see him for himself and not because she expected a free meal.

I could only have done this because I was in control of my finances. I had mastered the discipline of saving and growing my money. I was not a woman who spent a fortune buying shoes and clothes, and he respected me for it. My financial stability would later help us in building our relationship. We became partners, not just in life, but we also complemented each other in the businesses that we established.

A couple's values need to be aligned. You need to recognize and accept each other's flaws and resolve issues as soon as you can.

It's also important to have patience and an understanding of where each one is coming from. Love isn't just about emotion and sex; a life-long relationship is something that takes a lot of work from both sides. We were married in Canada in 1996, and we have adored each other every day since. We have two sons.

Four years later, I got an opportunity to help build Mary Kay Cosmetics in the Philippines. We intended to stay for a year or so. Unfortunately, I spent so much time selling to people who had no ability to pay that my business failed. It left us in a difficult financial situation.

Building from Scratch

I discovered that I didn't know anything about doing business in the Philippines. My only experience in the country was as a janitor or factory worker. I had a lot to learn. Gladly, my husband was there to get us back on track during a difficult time. I am always upset when I hear women talking so badly about men. Good men are great assets to women, and most men are good – or can be trained to be.

Richard and I partnered together to establish an executive search firm that would help expand the opportunities and incomes of Filipino leaders. Even though I didn't have a clue what CEOs were like in the Philippines, I called myself the CEO of Chalre Associates Executive Search. We helped huge international companies find senior leaders to run their operations in the country. Soon we found ourselves working for companies across Southeast Asia. It was so interesting dealing with senior managers from all over the world in diverse industries.

Richard and I were always upset when we went to other countries and people said such bad things about the Philippines. At the time, the reputation of the country was so bad that even Filipinos living in other countries spoke badly about it. And yet, when we spoke to international business people who were actually working here, they thought the Philippines, and especially Filipinos, were great.

That is the reason, we created Asia CEO Forum. We wanted to have a platform to display senior leaders doing great things for the country. It was set up specifically to be biased. We only showed good stories about the Philippines to counter all of the unfair bad stories that were endlessly repeated.

It became popular, and we now hold regular events for many different industries across the country. As speakers for our events, I have met and interviewed many of the most remarkable people of the nation's history, Presidents Marcos–Duterte–Ramos along with most of the biggest CEOs, Department Secretaries, Commissioners, and so on. For a little girl from Dasol, I never dreamed in my life I'd get to know these people.

We also launched Asia CEO Awards as a large-scale awards event to highlight the greatest leaders of the country and their amazing achievements. Today, Asia CEO Awards is said to be the largest event of its kind in Southeast Asia and attracts the elite of the nation and the region.

Maid to Made

I didn't imagine my story of rising against all odds would be noticed or of interest to anyone. But a journalist who attended our events asked to write an article about my story. She thought it would be an inspiration and source of strength to Filipinos. She came up with the phrase "Maid-to-Made," and the article she posted got 100,000 views in the first week.

That led to calls from many organizations for me to speak and tell my story to motivate their employees. I have since presented for amazing companies like Nestle, Google, American Express, Jollibee, Johnson

& Johnson, P&G, Insular Life, etc. They even fly me to countries like Singapore, Hong Kong, Malaysia, Japan, and Macau to speak to wonderful groups of up to 5,000 people.

News agencies have created so many feature programs about little me: CNN Philippines, Bloomberg, ABS-CBN, GMA, TV5, on and on. "Rated K" by Korina Sanchez did one that got 25 million views.

Promise Fulfilled

All that said, there is still lots to be done. I work 12 hours a day and will probably continue unless I get sick or can think of something else to do.

Looking back, I owe everything to my brothers and sisters. It was my need to support them that pushed me to keep working and growing. At such a young age, I had the responsibility to take care of them and send them to school.

Another important factor of my success is marrying the right husband. It is hard to build a career unless he is on your side and wants to help you.

In my book, "Maid to Made," I advise women to be meticulous in choosing their life partners because it's a critical factor for success. Having the same goals and vision, treating each other with trust and respect, and allowing each other space to grow are the ingredients to a strong and loving marriage.

Women should also share the same vision and values as their partners, especially on the meaning of family and their views on raising children.

Never lose your dreams. Write down your goals and save them on your phone. Take action toward them and have courage to think big. You will have many challenges, but think of these as trials and valuable learning experiences. Life is like climbing a mountain. It's tough. But once you reach the peak, the view is beautiful.

> **Never lose your dreams. Write down your goals and save them on your phone. Take action toward them and have courage to think big. You will have many challenges, but think of these as trials and valuable learning experiences. Life is like climbing a mountain. It's tough. But once you reach the peak, the view is beautiful.**

Develop good work habits. Maximize your time because time lost means lost opportunities. As a mother, I raised my children without nannies because Richard and I wanted to be role models for them. They saw how we worked, and they learned to be disciplined with their time and do chores on their own.

Be smart about your money. Save as much as you can and identify your priorities. In my case, my priority was saving for the future. After calculating what I needed to pay for the month, I put 20% to my savings. I suggest that women, especially overseas workers, be strict about saving their money. I know their families depend on them. But others need to share the burden by contributing too. You need to save your hard-earned money to prepare for your own future.

These days, I see many women spending fortunes on expensive clothes and bags. These are good for impressing your friends, but they don't help you achieve financial independence.

Love yourself. Love the people around you. Love what you do. Develop good relationships. Nurture your connections with those who have always been there for you, and life will be beautiful.

Develop respect and value the trust of others. Money can buy material things, but to have love, to have respect, to be trusted, these are the priceless things.

Philippine Dream

Always remember that you will be hit by many set-backs along the way. In 2005, I was diagnosed with a brain tumor, and the doctor told me I had only six months to live. I had lost most of my sight and could not walk.

I was brought back to Canada for medical treatment. I was surrounded by my loving family. The outpouring of support by friends and colleagues was overwhelming.

I followed a strict wellness regimen. My spirit didn't wane. I had been fighting all my life and had overcome seemingly impossible hurdles.

My body healed, and I recovered. My survival is one of the reasons why I want to give back to my country—by telling my story, doing acts of charity, and promoting the Philippines as a premier destination for investment and opportunities.

I'm a very positive person. But I do question myself when bad things happen. I ask myself if I made the right decisions. But I also turn my thoughts around and see the lesson behind the experience. That's what has also helped me survive despite all the challenges life has given me.

And so I believe, the more difficulties you face, the more grateful you should be. Overcoming obstacles is how you grow. If you don't have challenges, you're not growing.

Think of why these things are happening to you and say to yourself to keep going ahead. I've gone through so much, and even now, I always say keep going ahead.

I could have stopped working hard when I arrived in Canada. Instead, I chose to return to the Philippines and leave a richer and deeper legacy.

I have endured the worst of times: poverty, discrimination, horrible working conditions, a life-threatening tumor, and more. But I always chose to rise and be an example of hope to others.

My wish is to continue showing the world that with hope and a steadfast plan for one's dreams, you can achieve what you thought was unachievable. We are unbreakable more than we realize.

Six rules by Rebecca Bustamante

1. Never give up.
2. Give your best to everything you do.
3. Be faithful to God and be grateful for all the blessings in our life.
4. Keep fit and healthy.
5. Take care of your loved ones.
6. Mentor others to succeed in their lives.

Rebecca Bustamante

Keynote Speaker and Trainer

The life of Rebecca Bustamante started in extreme poverty. From a young age, she worked in homes wherever she would be fed. She left her home while still a teenager to work as a domestic helper in Singapore, working 24/7 with only one day off per month.

Motivational speakers and mentors inspire others to greatness because they themselves have led extraordinary lives. Rebecca provides practical, real life lessons anyone can use to improve their careers and life. She provides powerful presentations and mentorship across Philippines, Singapore, Malaysia, Japan, Hong Kong, Macao, Canada, and so on. Her moving speeches have been translated to Chinese, Japanese, Korean, and Indonesian.

Rebecca leaves people with a lasting sense that they can overcome any challenge and achieve any goal they desire. With Rebecca as your motivational speaker or executive coach, you will be brought to tears and stirred to inner joy while receiving the lessons of achievement that will stay with you for the rest of your lives.

Rebecca Bustamante develops in others the willpower, confidence, and capacity for hard-work necessary to both survive and succeed. She transfers her lessons in ways that are entertaining and touch people's hearts. Most of all, she transforms people's careers and personal lives in an enduring manner.

Kristine S. Calleja

BECOMING ME SLOWLY, PAINFULLY, GRATEFULLY

Let me begin my story with the death of my father seven years ago. He left us with a coffee and fruit orchard that he loved perhaps as much as his family. He was a farmer at heart, although he only had a farm when he was already 55. However, that didn't stop him from taking care of farm animals in our suburban home when I was growing up. He would even plant edibles at my mother's orchidarium and root crops in our garden. Sometimes, the ducks would decide to take a swim at our pool, and I would be asked to walk the goats in the afternoon.

In spite of my childhood experiences, I hardly know a thing or two about farming. It was never my passion until I was left to care for the farm. We could have sold it when my father passed away but not trying to care for it would have been a dishonor to him. I needed to at least try. But like most of my interests, it started with a struggle. I kept on because, from experience, I knew it gets better over time.

Taking over the farm, I thought I was just going to continue my father's legacy. But it was proving to be a burdensome task year after year because my heart was not in it. I had to learn to love it, and I had to love it fast. I would not have enough finances for another year if I remain uninspired. What I needed was a spark. That spark came in the form of a friend from long ago.

My friend messaged me out of the blue one day in 2022. She wanted to share with me something she thought I could do on the farm. We were in the middle of the Covid-19 pandemic, and like most people our age, she fell in love with gardening. Because of gardening, she learned about composting. She wanted me to try bokashi, a Japanese composting system of fermenting food waste and turning it into compost in only four weeks. At first, I was skeptical, but I have such high regard for that friend that I said yes. Unbeknownst to me, that yes turned out to be the spark that would change my view of the farm forever.

Before I only thought of growing coffee and fruits, and maybe some vegetables and flowers. But when I learned to make kompashi or compost from bokashi, I recognized the potential of the farm as an eco-hub or, better yet, as an eco-village. I could now finally connect the farm to the city and back, with the city supplying the food waste and the farm processing it into compost and utilizing the compost as an input in food production. I saw a truly circular economy. My heart was finally hooked on the idea.

With a renewed sense of purpose, I started meeting people with the same passion and the same dreams. My friend introduced me to a social entrepreneur for bokashi, and she, in turn, introduced me to other people in the world of farming and composting. Suddenly, my world became much bigger and brighter with everyone's intense passions and immense dreams.

Many lives, many worlds

Before I had to manage the farm, I had other lives. I still do. I am a writer, researcher, and advocacy strategist. I wear so many hats that I often feel stumped whenever I have to introduce myself. Not that I do not know what to say. I just do not know where to begin.

When I was 25, I received a call from a government office asking if I had ever written a speech before. Recalling I had written one speech in my life before that time, I said yes. My yes must have sounded confident because the woman on the other line invited me to take a writing test and interview soon afterward. I suppose I passed the test and interview because I was hired. That government office turned out to be the Speechwriting Office for the President of the Philippines. At 25, I became the youngest presidential speechwriter at that time.

When I was 35, I woke up one day to the thought that perhaps I should try my hand at advocacy, knowing how much I loved politics. After battling a stormy cloud of depression for several months, I searched the job openings for an advocacy position. Lo and behold, there was an opening for that position in an international non-governmental organization (INGO). I did not hesitate and applied for the job. I had zero background in advocacy work, but I had government experience and confidence in my ability to learn on the job. I was pitted against candidates who had INGO experience and PhDs. But we all had to undergo the same test and the same interview process. Somehow, luck favored me, and I got the job.

The first year when I was still learning advocacy work, I leaned on my communication background. But by the second year, I found my footing. Part of my work was to get a treatment protocol for severe acute malnutrition institutionalized in the Philippines. I did not only help get the protocol approved but also got the Philippines to become a signatory to the global multi-sector campaign, Scaling Up Nutrition.

I feel like I have lived many lives, crisscrossed many paths, and undergone many journeys – even when in reality I am just 46. I think what has driven and continues to drive me to this day is my relentless, untiring, and, undoubtedly when I was younger, reckless curiosity. Curiosity is one thing that ties all these lives and worlds together, and it is the one thing that has kept it from falling apart.

Boundless curiosity

I was a very curious child, but TV mostly bored me, particularly cartoons and children's shows. I only felt I had to watch them because that's what my elder brother did and that's what I thought children do. If I had had my way, I would have been outdoors, exploring, or in a corner, reading a book.

At five years old, I taught myself how to ride a two-wheeled bike with my father's bike. If I sat on the bike, I could not even reach the pedals. So I asked our *kasambahay* to sit on the bike while I pedaled standing up. The following year, I taught myself how to swim. I observed that when dogs fall into the water, they float. So I thought humans might too. Despite my fear of drowning, I went into the pool sans my floaters and discovered I too could float naturally.

I liked to observe animals and mimic them. From watching cats every afternoon, I learned how to jump from a high place and land on the hard floor without injuring myself. When I got into accidents, I would lick my wounds as dogs do. That is how I discovered that blood had iron because it tasted like metal on my tongue.

No, I am not a prodigy. I was not even an early reader. I was already six when I started to read. I remember the first word I ever read in my life. One afternoon, I stopped and stared at the lock hanging on our walk gate. I was very curious to know what the four letters engraved on the lock were. I started making the sound: "y… a… l… e…," and then after several attempts, magic: ya... le...." But it probably took me several more afternoons to figure out it was pronounced "Yale."

However, once I learned to read, I became a voracious reader. I kept borrowing books from the library and reading at home. By the time I was in high school, I was elected president of the library club. However, reading did not come naturally to me. I would often catch myself misreading a word, jumping over it, or interchanging its sequence. It happened often enough that I developed a way to catch it through logic. What I am reading has to make sense. When it does not, I read it over and over until I get its logic.

Aside from being a terrible reader, I was also a terrible speller. I know it is surprising because I became a writer, an accidental one to be exact. One day when I was in junior high, my friends and I wanted to skip our physical education class. We ended up taking a test for the school paper. Lucky me, I got it. The following year, I was promoted to features editor. I also received the journalism award at our high school graduation. By college, I was taking up literature, writing for our literary folio, and receiving a writing award for fiction.

In 2022, after over 30 years, my English teacher in freshman high school messaged me, asking if I could read her book. I was surprised. I wanted to ask her, "Why me?" But I was too shy to ask. I think she read my mind when she said, "You know, you are the best writer in your batch." I almost cried. I don't think she remembered she gave me a C in English.

It is not true though that I fell in love with books when I learned to read because I had already fallen in love with books long before I could read. I learned to read because I yearned to know what was in those books. I still remember the first book I was fascinated with. It was the first volume of a ten-volume children's encyclopedia, and it featured a Cro-Magnon inside the Cave of Altamira on its cover. To this day, I am fascinated with history to the point of taking it as a minor for my literature degree in college.

Adversity quotient

If there is something I am very familiar with, it is adversity. I have suffered from depression as long as I can remember. When I was six, I watched my stomach rise and fall while sitting at the foot of my parents' bed. I wondered how many more breaths of air I would take before taking in my last. When I became sick the following year, I felt so at peace at the thought that perhaps I could finally die. My troubled teens came a decade ahead. That's why I know how to work hard for something because, more than I care to admit, I have worked hard to stay alive for a very long time now.

"
That's why I know how to work hard for something because, more than I care to admit, I have worked hard to stay alive for a very long time now.

What kept the suicidal ideations at bay was not so much my grit as my curiosity. The intensity of my curiosity was my adversity quotient. The more I am intellectually and emotionally engaged, the more I am able to surmount my difficulties. My curiosity carried me through the toughest of times. I always wanted to know what was on the other side of my darkness. Is it finally light? Strangely enough, the thought gave me hope.

But the darkness was unabating. I had to finally see a psychiatrist. In 2008, I was diagnosed with major depressive disorder, and two years later, with bipolar disorder. Although the medicines gave me relief, I never got off them. I kept switching, adding, and switching medications whenever my depression was too much to handle. I felt there was something more to me.

Although it crossed my mind that I could be on the autism spectrum long before the publication of DSM V, I was too afraid to seek a diagnosis. I was concerned that I would be dismissed. My concern was not unfounded. When I finally tried to get a diagnosis in 2020 and 2021, several doctors did dismiss me. They refused to even consider my symptoms. One asked why I wanted to get a diagnosis when I was functional. I guess, for him, wanting to know myself was not enough. Another said he would only diagnose me when I was no longer depressed, as depression can mimic the autism spectrum. But I have always been depressed. Does that mean I would never qualify for a diagnosis?

In 2022, I went to see a sleep doctor who is also a psychiatrist. I wanted to wean myself off sleeping pills and was asking her how I should go about it. She said that my sleep cycle is in reverse. I should be asleep during the day and awake at night if I wanted to rid myself of the sleeping pills. But since I was also taking care of my mother during the day who had had a stroke in 2016, I decided to follow the neurotypical sleep cycle and continue to take a sleeping pill at night. But the good thing that came out of that consultation with her was the diagnosis I had been waiting for.

After several more visits to her clinic, I was finally diagnosed with the autism spectrum with ADHD in 2023. Like most adults diagnosed with autism spectrum, the diagnosis came as a relief. It gave validation to my suspicion that my difference from the norm lay somewhere more fundamental to my being. I don't act typical because I am not neurotypical. Being diagnosed to be on the autism spectrum has allowed me to rediscover my neurodivergence.

Surrendering to my becoming

Today, I am nurturing my becoming. Being comfortable in my own skin has given me the opportunity to explore the things I thought I could not do because I could not do them the same way other people do. I used to be very uncomfortable in front of people and would often shy away from public speaking. But once I started doing it the way I feel comfortable, I realized I do not only enjoy sharing knowledge, I desire it. Although I would still prefer to be behind the scenes, I can already bring down my guard and relax on stage.

For a long time, I thought I was alone in my journey, and that was okay. I thought that I could discover things on my own and that I did not need anyone to guide me through my journey. I thought people were only there to tell me what to do as if that is the only thing that people are meant to do for each other. I was wrong. People are there for a reason. Sometimes, we are crossing paths and coming from different journeys, while other times we are embarking on the same journeys. We just need to be open to each other and see and recognize in each other that we are all merely becoming ourselves, hopefully, our best versions.

This is what happened when I met my co-founders of the Academy of Green Industries and Living Ecosystems (AGILE). We crossed paths because of our interest in and advocacy for ecological justice, and we embarked on a journey together as partners because we can do more for ecological justice if we are together than we ever could if we were apart. Our advocacy work immediately bore fruit. We were advancing a development framework in our city when an office in our city government adopted it in their strategy. Our campaign has now become much bigger and stronger.

That development framework is the social solidarity economy (SSE). An ethical and values-based approach to socio-economic development, SSE prioritizes the well-being of people and the planet. Moreover, SSE seeks to transform our social and economic system from an orientation toward profit to that toward shared prosperity.

Going beyond helping the poor and marginalized, SSE strives to overcome inequalities, addressing fundamental issues with the active participation of ordinary people in shaping all dimensions of human life -- from social to cultural, political, economic, and environmental.

Being curious has not only allowed me to experience serendipities, but it also gives me the burning desire to go past my darkness to see the light, and in the process, discover myself. I am often amazed that I am able to cope and later thrive. If before I said over and over "I can do this" whenever I was struggling with something, today I can finally say I am good at this now that I trust my own becoming.

"Being curious has not only allowed me to experience serendipities, but it also gives me the burning desire to go past my darkness to see the light, and in the process, discover myself.

In the hyperrealist painting "Surrender," multimedia artist Rebie Ramoso depicts a woman underwater. Her head is not visible in the painting, suggesting that only her body is submerged and her head is above water. Clad in a white nightgown, the woman seems relaxed after a long struggle. The painting suggests she could be drowning or merely floating calmly, naturally. Either way, she is in surrender. The last seven years of my life has been a struggle with the person I am becoming. But now I am in complete surrender.

Kristine Calleja

An advocate for social and ecological justice as well as gender equality, Tin is a feminist social entrepreneur. Her work is centered on co-creating ways of organizing people, resources, and systems toward a just, equitable, and abundant world. She sits on the board of several local and international nonprofits and social enterprises that share her advocacy and vision.

She is the President of CalleMon EcoVillage, and is the co-founder of the sustainability consultancy network Academy of Green Industries and Living Ecosystems (AGILE).

For over two decades, she has been working as a policy advocacy strategist and strategic communication specialist in the government and non-government sectors as well as in local and transnational corporations, with the aim of understanding and transforming the dynamics of power to lean towards the poor and marginalized.

She is a long-time writer and researcher, having written in various publications in the Philippines and abroad. She is one of the lead authors of the Philippine NGO Beijing + 25 Report published in March 2020.

http://linkedin.com/in/kscalleja.

Ma. Rhodora "Ayhee" Campos

My Thirteen-Word Life Lesson in a Three-Part Story

If I had pronounced my nickname right when I was a child, I would have been known as the fictional blue tang and one of the major characters of the animated film series "Finding Nemo." My nickname should have been "Dory," but I can only pronounce vowels. So it ended as *Ayi*. Unlike Dory who suffered from short-term memory loss but was known for her childlike optimism and ability to communicate in different languages, "Ayhee" is known for her courage, grit, and purpose.

If I were to write a straightforward story of my life, the simplest version might go like this: My name is Ayhee Campos. I am a people leader for the past twenty-seven years, where 24 years were spent in the IT-BPM space. I am a licensed medical technologist. I am mother to two beautiful children – Luis and Patricia – and a wife to Leo. I saw opportunities coming my way. Doors opened – first one, then another – and I walked through them.

By having my story told in one of the chapters in this book, I will share the lessons that have helped me live a sentient life. It will be segmented – and overlapping at the same time – into three chapters: Explorer, Builder, and Navigator. Each chapter inspired me to face the challenges over the years and gave me a deeper understanding of myself and the world around me.

Explorer

Our family has a strong bond. I am the eldest of two siblings. My mother is a dedicated homemaker, and my father is an accountant. My father wanted me to become a doctor. His opinion mattered. That's why I took up Medical Technology. It was an aspiration for parents to see their children carry a title in their names. In my case, a prefix with the letters D and R would have been their ultimate dream. In the same way I mispronounced my supposed nickname and missed the consonants in it, my father's dream of seeing his daughter become a doctor didn't become a reality.

It is almost impossible to explain how our life went because of a major financial imbroglio which led to us selling our house. This was followed by my father getting ill. He suffered a stroke, almost died, stayed months in the hospital, and was bedridden for 14 years. This made my brother, my mother, me, and especially my father feel helpless and defenseless. My mom leveraged her excellent cooking skills, delivering meals for friends and relatives while I sold street food in front of our small apartment, all while taking care of my father. I have always been an intuitive person. Knowing that there is competition selling the same products along the street, I concocted a secret sauce for our fish balls, squid balls, and kikiam, and we would always sell faster than the others. My brother, on the other hand, left the seminary for an opportunity to work in the U.S. so he could help support our father.

Around that time, I remember having the strangest feeling. Life was telling me something, and the message was very clear. It was a wake-up call as to whether I wanted to see what life had to offer. Or I could hop back on the hamster wheel. My new focus was to pronounce all the vowels and consonants and make a conscious effort to change the conversation in my head. Even today, I do this over and over again. Every single day, I meditate and pray. I was seized by the thought that we all needed protection. I also knew that my next steps would affect me and my family directly. My family has been my anchor and my safe space – I can't let them down. Somehow, although I didn't know how, I knew I had to find a way.

So, I prayed for clarity of mind, strength, and guidance to find my purpose and my next steps. I asked to be shown the way. One day, I got an answer from a friend: customer service at a local telecommunications company. At the time, I wasn't sure if it was the right answer. All I said was thank you. My prayer was heard, and I was shown a path to take.

Life is magical. Being a medical technologist in a customer service world is the perfect failure equation. But truly I was happy to be there.

In 1994, as a *contractual* telephone operator in a conglomerate, I could finally say that I had a place in this world. It certainly wasn't a straight shot. But I was getting started.

Every day was hectic at work. When I think about my daily schedule, I realize that almost every day felt like a ritual, and I really wanted to create something new for myself. I may have finished my tasks for the day, but I would always check for new opportunities to learn. So, I would speak to my direct supervisor to mentor me and work on additional projects. After three months, I was promoted, on a probationary status, as Department Clerk/Secretary to the Manager of Customer Service.

Navigating the corporate world was unlike the medical laboratory I had become used to. In a laboratory, I was the one in control of analyzing a variety of biological specimens. Now, it felt like I was one of the specimens being watched and evaluated. Sitting in silence, I asked myself, "*Is this the job my father would have wanted me to have?*" In my mind, my father would have already given me the answer. He used to tell me to "take a leap of faith." This job is an answered prayer, and I knew that my father – being the nurturer that he was – whispered to the Almighty to make this situation an opportunity in which I could thrive.

As a Department Clerk/Secretary, I had to do tasks that I had zero knowledge of and had not experienced in my life. Take, for example, using a computer, project management, understanding financials, and speaking the English language fluently. But I had to do all of them or else I would fail myself and my family. I needed the discipline to learn. Having discipline isn't always easy. And what is the best way to start? To have self-awareness. Yet having self-awareness is a process. I didn't have a clue about corporate life. That's why I needed to learn because I was aware that I could do more. Yet, for me to deepen and expand my capabilities, I knew I could not do it alone. I needed help. Then I sought mentors, and I wasn't ashamed to ask for help from my peers who knew more. I grew in that company, was promoted several times and when I left after almost four years, I was already a senior supervisor, responsible for Provincial Operations.

Builder

Everything starts as a dream. But first, you need to know what your dream is and why you want it. I have always wanted to become a people manager. I developed my work ethic by sharing a small house with my mother, brother, and father. We were a very small family. I watched my parents work as hard as they did. Being the eldest – and losing my father – I became disciplined, courageous, and receptive. That's why it was easy for me to be strong inside and be adaptive to the energy of other people around me, which I believe would make me a great people manager.

After being with the local telecommunications company for almost four years, I moved to a global telecommunications company as Junior Manager. I was responsible for setting up Hotline Operations. But after two months in that role, I was moved to set up and lead a new department called Fulfillment Operations. I built the team and process from the ground up. I was sent to the U.S. for training since the role was new in the country.

A big part of me continued to explore the ins and outs of the role. If something was scaring me, I knew it was up to me to work through my fears and doubts. If I wanted to do more in this role, I had to work double or triple more that I was currently doing. It didn't matter that I didn't know something. It didn't matter how long I had to sit in front of my desktop to develop a strategy on how we could enable our sales teams and help drive the growth of the company. It didn't matter how frightened I was that the strategy might not work. My bigger purpose this time was self-investment. I had to learn to make it work. It wasn't about me anymore. I was responsible for the people reporting to me, and they had to see me walk the talk.

Then the next challenges became a little harder, but I knew I had to rise to meet them. Every single one of them. The next was much harder than the other. This helped me develop patience, and it gave me the rush and the necessary strength to go on. It eventually helped build my confidence. Let's face it, at some point, my emotions could have overtaken me completely. It can easily define us or limit our potential; my self-doubt would have paralyzed me. Instead, I focused my attention on what I wanted to accomplish. Then, I got pregnant with my first child. The focus suddenly was divided into motherhood and/or career. I was lucky to have a very strong support system which allowed me to pursue both together. A few months later, before I gave birth, I was introduced to the sunrise industry of the country – Contact Center/BPO.

It turned out that walking away from this global telecommunications company was the start of my IT-BPM career. It was in 2000 that I joined one of the pioneer BPO companies in the country. It was an emerging industry that had taken many small steps. Good for me, for the country. To my mind though, this would require immense dedication. I was pregnant and about to give birth in a few months. How would I be able to balance motherhood and be a Program Manager for one of the Fortune 100 companies? This was when I started to realize that balance is relative. I wouldn't be able to divide 24 hours equally. I would need a team, not only in the office but also at home. I was very thankful for my husband who was so generous in allowing me to pursue my career, my mom who looked after our nanny, and of course, the nanny who took care of my son like he was her own. In my career, this was the time, I started building my teams too. One account, then two, until it became a business unit and later on a site plus more.

> **“When I think back to the words my mentors have said to me and what I learned from my teams, those were the words and experiences that inspired me, motivated me, frightened me, and made me feel loved and appreciated. Some words hurt me. Some nurtured me. Some pushed me. It made me ready for what was coming next.**

I would like to believe that I had found the biggest pieces of my puzzle when I joined the company. It was a powerful, beautiful, and rewarding eight years. I was fully present while growing with the company. When I think back to the words my mentors have said to me and what I learned from my teams, those were the words and experiences that inspired me, motivated me, frightened me, and made me feel loved and appreciated. Some words hurt me. Some nurtured me. Some pushed me. It made me ready for what was coming next.

In this chapter, my self-awareness became stronger. Until then, I had always reminded myself to make an effort to know myself better – my strengths and my opportunities to always be the better version of myself every day. This allowed me to focus on my whys and whats to make daily progress.

But as I saw myself growing further in my career, I gave birth to our second child, which had some major complications – pre eclampsia that resulted in internal bleeding and a long hospitalization. I was given a 30/70 chance of survival. I was in and out of a coma, 21 days in ICU, and few months in the hospital. I almost gave up, but one morning, I woke up. My husband had posted pictures of my children on the walls and played some church songs. Luis was one-and-a-half years old and Patricia was a one-month old infant. It reminded me how beautiful life was. I prayed to GOD to heal me to my old self so I could take care of my babies and my parents – my bedridden dad and aging mother. The whole process was revealed to me, Almighty's miracle. I was removed from the respirator, and I started to breathe on my own again. Throughout the ordeal, we were accompanied by our dear family and friends.

In 2008, I decided to take a different path, and I joined one of the largest and oldest IT companies in the Philippines. It was an exciting journey for almost two years – exploring and building at the same time. I came from a company founded in the Philippines and was fortunate to be part of the pioneering teams. This time, I was joining a global organization where the Philippines was just one of the many countries they operated in. I needed to learn to navigate a matrix organization while I built one of the business units. I faced different kinds of challenges, but at the end of the day, hard work, perseverance, humility always worked! I decided to take a break from corporate, and I went on sabbatical for a year to support my husband as he dabbled in business. I also thought, this was the best time to spend time with the kids. We relocated to Cebu during this period.

Navigator

I was happy to give this break a chance. Growing up in a small family taught me to appreciate my values, experience endless gratitude, or simply eat dinner together. I think Leo – *my husband* – and I achieved what we were aiming to do. After a year of building a family in Cebu, we chose to go back to our life in Manila.

I joined a local company in 2011, and I got excited at the idea of making a local brand thrive in the midst of global brands in the country. But, my intent and the direction of the company didn't align; hence, I decided to move on. In 2012, I joined a global company, Infosys BPM. I was hired to lead the CS practice/delivery in Philippines, but it was the same story as my previous stints in other companies. After a few months, I was tasked to lead the branch, as the country head. Here I was tasked to build the team, grow the company by driving delivery excellence, and create a positive impression to our global sales teams and clients regarding the country and the delivery center.

During this time, I was invited to run for a board seat in two industry associations enabling the IT-BPM Industry. I am grateful to the different industry leaders who gave me their vote and the opportunity to serve our beloved industry. I am on my third term as BOT for IBPAP (IT-BPM Association of the Philippines) and am now serving as Vice Chair while I've finish my two terms in CCAP (Contact Association of the Philippines), serving as a board adviser. Recently, I represented IBPAP and was elected as Board and Vice President for Go Digital Pilipinas, a movement driving the country's digitization agenda.

Last year, my role in Infosys was expanded beyond the Philippines. I was tasked to set up and lead Malaysia DC for Infosys, with the charter being very similar to the Philippines: expand and grow a presence in Malaysia. I was also honored to have been appointed to be a member of Infosys's Leadership Council where I get the opportunity to participate in navigating the next phase of the organization.

In my 12th year as a #KaInfoscion**, our journey continues *to amplify human potential and create opportunities for people, businesses, and communities.*

I am navigating both inside the company and the industry. At the same time, I continue to explore and build.

You may have heard the story about the crow and the pitcher. It's a classic Aesop's fable, and it goes like this: A thirsty crow comes across a pitcher, which had been full of water. But when she put her beak into the mouth of the pitcher, she couldn't reach the water. She kept trying but then gave up. At last, she had an idea. She kept dropping pebbles into the pitcher, and soon the water rose to the top. Finally, she quenched her thirst.

I can relate to this story – it's simple and deep. I still think about it every time I see myself at a crossroads and on a quest to realign with my purpose in life. It took both courage and grit to act on the idea to drop the pebbles. I wanted to persevere, lead through change with authenticity and passion, and inspire others – *especially women* – in remarkable circumstances. Though at times, I feel like the more I learn, the less I know. But there are some things that never change, the greatest lesson about having a lifelong sense of purpose will make you dream big and brave.

"
I wanted to persevere, lead through change with authenticity and passion, and inspire others – especially women – in remarkable circumstances. Though at times, I feel like the more I learn, the less I know. But there are some things that never change, the greatest lesson about having a lifelong sense of purpose will make you dream big and brave.

My story is about exploring to learn what I didn't know, add value by building what I could, and lead by navigating to the next stage – all anchored on my life's purpose, which I have defined in various stages of both my personal and professional life.

Whatever path I choose, I have my thirteen-word guide as a reminder: With courage, grit, and purpose, one can do what others say you can't!

* At Infosys, we do not call our people employees, we call them Infoscions.

** *Ka* is a Filipino prefix that means you belong to a bigger family and KaInfoscion means that you are part of the bigger Infosys BPM Philippines community. KaInfoscion has evolved to be the employee-value proposition of Infosys BPM Philippines.

Ma. Rhodora "Ayhee" Campos

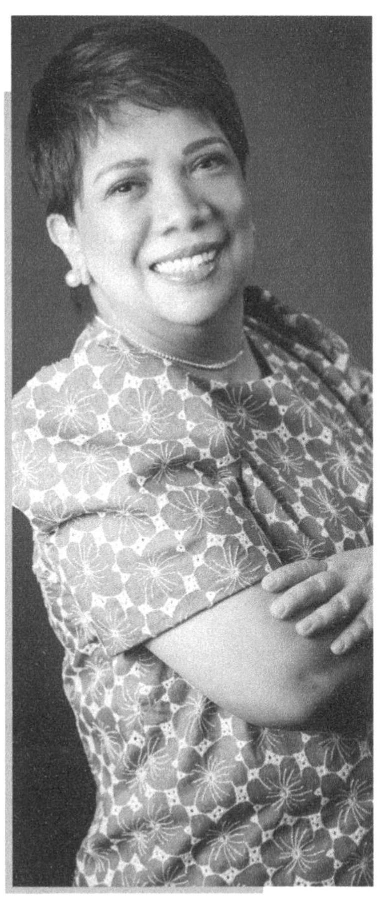

Country Head and Senior Regional Delivery Center Head, Infosys BPM Philippines and Malaysia
Explorer • Builder • Navigator

Ma. Rhodora "Ayhee" Campos serves as the Country Head and Senior Regional Delivery Center Head ofInfosys BPM in the Philippines and Malaysia. In this role, Ayhee is responsible for overall operations,transformation initiatives, and increasing the Infosys BPM footprint. She is a member of the Infosys BPMLeadership Council where she participates in problem-solving and strategy execution on critical businessimperatives across the Infosys BPM global organization. She also leads the diversity efforts for the Asia Pacificregion.

Ayhee brings 26 years of rich leadership experience and intensive domain capability. She played multipleroles spanning telecommunications, customer service, and business process outsourcing. She was aBusiness Unit Head at Accenture and the President and Chief Operating Officer at Pacific Hub.

A firm practitioner in balancing the Head and Heart quotient, Ayhee is a #KaInfoscion leader known forbringing the Infosys brand of innovation and excellence in reimagining business processes and peoplemanagement. She is an advocate for diversity, equity, and belongingness; a proponent of continuouslearning and development; and passionate about strengthening the Philippine IT-BPM industry to remainglobally competitive and relevant.

A well-rounded industry leader, Ayhee was awarded the Global Filipino Executive Leader of the Year andCircle of Excellence Woman Leader of the Year by the Asia CEO in 2023. She is the Vice Chairperson of the IT-BPM Association of the Philippines (IBPAP) in her third term. She just finished her second term as a

BoardDirector for the Contact Center Association of the Philippines (CCAP) and is now one of CCAP's BoardAdvisers. Ayhee is the convenor and chairperson of Women In Action (WIA) at IT-BPM. She is also a Board ofDirector of Go Pilipinas, representing the IT-BPM industry.

She was a UN Women Asia-Pacific WEP Gold Awardee on Leadership (2022) and was named by the FilipinaWomen's Network (FWN) as one of the 100 Most Influential Filipina Women in the World (2014). She is amember of the Management Association of the Philippines (MAP) and Filipina CEO Circle (FCC).

Laurice Chiongbian

Unleashing Grit: Reflections From a Former Impost-her's Entrepreneurial Journey

Entrepreneurship is living a few years of your life like most people won't so that you can spend the rest of your life like most people can't."
~ Anonymous

"Entrepreneurship is not just about creating a company; it's about creating a mindset."
~ Brian Chesky (founder of Airbnb)

The Alchemy of Entrepreneurship

What does it take to be an entrepreneur? If you're an entrepreneur, you know that success begins with your ability to spot market opportunities. But what if you're not an expert in your industry? Don't worry, because according to Paul Graham, the founder of Y Combinator, you don't need to be: "Entrepreneurship is the art of finding profitable solutions to problems." In fact, many entrepreneurs become successful by venturing beyond their field of expertise and exploring new markets.

In 2016, I started my first company, Qavalo, Inc. Armed only with a clear vision and zero industry experience in outsourcing or the US home health industry, I set out on the most fulfilling professional pursuit of my life. So how do you get comfortable with a new market? The key is to network with potential customers and industry partners. Don't be afraid to step out of your comfort zone and strike up conversations with people who can give you insights into your market. The more you know about your potential customers, the more confident and comfortable you'll be when pitching your ideas.

Persuasiveness is essential, but it must be genuine. **If you want to earn the trust of your potential customers, you need to develop a persuasive voice for your industry.** That means speaking their language, understanding their pain points, and presenting your solutions in a way that resonates with them.

So, be open to opportunities and conversations about your industry. You never know where they might lead.

Develop a strong work routine to combat imposter syndrome

Always show up to work, even if there aren't any customers. As a female entrepreneur, let me be among the first to tell you—imposter syndrome is real. But the good news is that it's not insurmountable. According to a survey conducted by The Second Shift, 67% of female entrepreneurs experience imposter syndrome. However, a meta-analysis of studies on the "imposter phenomenon" suggests that "fake it till you make it" strategies, such as acting confident or competent, can help individuals overcome feelings of inadequacy and perform better in their roles. **Establishing a strong work routine early on, even if there isn't much work to do yet, can help you maintain build confidence and focus when things pick up.** When Qavalo was just starting out and had no clients, I made it a point to show up to work on time every day and mentally prepare for whatever tasks or problems might come my way. Not only did this set an important tone for my growing team, but it also helped me develop a clear hierarchy of priorities that has been invaluable as the business has grown.

> **"I made it a point to show up to work on time every day and mentally prepare for whatever tasks or problems might come my way. Not only did this set an important tone for my growing team, but it also helped me develop a clear hierarchy of priorities that has been invaluable as the business has grown.**

Co-working space for all the right reasons

Fortunately, by the time I started Qavalo in 2016, a strong first wave of entrepreneurs had arrived in Cebu and introduced the concept of the co-working space. Locating our initial operations here proved to be instrumental to our success for the obvious reasons that it was cost-effective and centrally-located but also carried a surprising additional benefit—unknowing applicants came into the space and thought that the whole place was ours! Around the time that we signed our third and by far our largest client, we had to fill twelve spots urgently to meet our promised start date. We learned later that many of the applicants turned employees thought that all 300 people on the floor were employees of Qavalo, and because of this were able to sell the idea of working for a startup to some would-be skeptics. The fact remains that the Philippines workforce is still very risk averse and no one goes into the healthcare field because they are wired for high-risk high rewards. Most of these applicants were steered into the healthcare profession by familial pressure to earn and prioritize job security, so the semblance of an established organization was vital. I can only imagine their surprise when they found out we, in fact, only leased three rows of desks and not the entire floor! But by that point, they were willing to stick it out, and that trust motivated us to also put a timeline in place to have our own office as soon as it was financially feasible.

The Power of Exercise in Enhancing Executive Function

Exercise is more than just a physical activity. It has been proven to have a positive effect on executive function, cognitive function, attention, and processing speed.

Moreover, physical activity is known to reduce stress and anxiety levels, leading to better mental health. As a startup founder, I found exercise to be a crucial tool in managing the demands of entrepreneurship. In my first year of starting Qavalo, I became a spin instructor. The intense cardio and weight training I did helped me manage stress and gave me clarity and focus. By prioritizing exercise and making it a part of my daily routine, I was able to compartmentalize my stress and improve my efficiency, which is critical to a lean and iterative startup mindset. I packed my lunches and snack boxes the night before, went into our co-working space for a full day of work, then headed straight to the studio for a spin session or teacher's training. **The focused nature of teaching forced me to prioritize efficiency over perfection**, which has been a valuable lesson in my entrepreneurial journey.

The power of early wins for startups

First client: I still remember when we signed our first client. I had hired someone to do outbound sales, and while he knew nothing about healthcare or outsourcing, he wasn't shy to get on the phone. His affable charm must have come across over the phone because he managed to convince a small, yet well-established, agency to give outsourcing a try. I couldn't believe it! Of course, as any first time entrepreneur would do, I did the straight math and foolishly computed that at this rate we would be scaling 12 x our first year! Of course client acqusiition never is that simple, but I'll never forget the huge boost that was to our spirits. **A quick, early win was all the validation we needed to keep us going through what would be a very exhilarating and exhausting first year in operation.** That client also stayed with us for six years until their eventual acquisition during Covid by a larger company. We are always grateful for the faith and trust in us from the get-go.

Navigating growth in the early days : Biting off more than we can chew

Within weeks of signing our first client, we signed two more, much larger in size and had to 20x our production staff. Those were stressful times, trying to hire, train, and manage at a rate we were not prepared for. Looking back, it was helpful that we didn't have to deal with facilities constraints (the co-working space was very flexible and accommodating), and we had always been very honest and open with our clients about the fact that we were just starting out. There were components of that quick ramp-up that we never quite figured out, and we were able to learn quickly by failing fast. We learned what types of clients were the most profitable, that shorter episodes meant faster turnover, meant more work for us and smaller margins. We learned that the bottlenecks in growth would quickly become the clinical talent. But also, **we quickly cultivated a mindset for growth and learning,** and our core team that adopted quickly to this mindset are still with us today.

Learning from the Experts: Building a Strong Support Network for Your Business

The importance of having subject matter experts as part of your network cannot be overstated. These are individuals who have extensive experience and expertise in a particular field and can provide valuable insights and guidance. In the early stages of Qavalo, the founders recognized the importance of having access to such experts and proactively built a network of industry veterans. This network proved invaluable in providing perspective on the industry, identifying real industry problems, and ultimately helping to inform Qavalo's product and service offerings.

In addition, it is crucial to surround yourself with individuals who are smarter than you. As an entrepreneur or business owner, it can be easy to fall into the trap of thinking that you know everything and that you can handle every aspect of your business. However, this is rarely the case. By surrounding yourself with people who are more knowledgeable or experienced in certain areas than you are, you can leverage their skills and expertise to improve your business. Not only can they help you identify blind spots or areas where you need improvement, but they can also bring fresh ideas and new perspectives to the table. This approach can be particularly effective in the fast-paced and ever-changing world of startups, where adaptability and innovation are key to success.

The importance of an entrepreneur's network extends beyond the organization. A study published in the journal Nature found that an individual's success is strongly influenced by the success of their immediate social network. Specifically, the study found that **a person's chance of becoming successful increases by 3% for every successful connection in their network**. One essential key to success is to surround yourself with the right people. Avoiding the negative influences of naysayers and unmotivated individuals can prevent doubt and help maintain motivation towards achieving one's goals.

THE FEAR OF LOSING MY EDGE: NAVIGATING PREGNANCY AS A CEO

One essential key to success is to surround yourself with the right people. Avoiding the negative influences of naysayers and unmotivated individuals can prevent doubt and help maintain motivation towards achieving one's goals.

We found out we were expecting our third child almost exactly one year to the day I started working on Qavalo. It was April 2017, and I felt like I had been running a marathon that had no finish line in sight. I felt a lot of pressure about how to break the news to my team. Would they judge me for being tired all the time? Would they chalk my moods up to pregnancy hormones? Would I lose my edge? I felt strongly that my first year as a CEO had been defined by my ability to successfully juggle so much at once: work, exercise, strict diet regimen, the demands of being a pretty involved mother to my two, and a director at my husband's company. Within the Qavalo organization itself that first year, I wore multiple hats (as most founders do), guiding marketing and operations very closely. I chose to wait until the end of my first trimester before I shared the news. I wanted to come out as strong as possible in those first three months and afford myself the breathing space to take it easier later in the pregnancy. Sure enough, with construction of the new office and the mounting personnel issues, work made sure to get its fill of me. During those months, we were still doing lead verification calls on U.S. time, and I would often go into the co-working space late at night to help keep our marketing officer motivated, since he was oftentimes the only person left at the office. During the day, I would inspect the construction site and put in lots of face time with the day shift staff. We were still understanding how to build rapport with our U.S. clients, so I would shadow zoom meetings and sometimes step in if I felt like the relationships had to be reinforced. All the while, I still kept up my cycling workout regimen, although I did stop teaching. Looking back, it looks like I was just doing too much and any one misstep could have thrown the whole thing into chaos, but at the time, it all felt like the most perfectly calibrated dance, with one side perfectly balancing the other mentally and physically, I felt at my peak performance and sharpness.

An office of our own

Our first office was bare bones. No Google-esque foosball tables or unlimited snack room. But in keeping it practical, there was also a communal sense of achievement when we finally did move into our own space, almost one year to the day after we started the company. At that point, we had grown to a team of about 45 people, and the victory of being one of the first teams to graduate from the co-working space was palpable. Nonetheless, the move also meant more administrative demands on our team and overhead costs, as we now had to manage our own facilities and utilities, including the internet. Despite this, I was mindful of selecting an affordable space with room to grow within the building. Over the next year, we expanded by adding two more units on different floors, which wasn't the most convenient set-up, but it gave us flexibility without financial strain. Those were some of our happiest days, moving between floors with the same excitement as if we owned the whole building. While the growth phase held promise and optimism for the organization, it was my responsibility as CEO to manage expectations and keep everyone on task. At times, it felt challenging to balance enthusiasm and focus, but **helping the team find gratification in working for each and every notch on our belts in a healthy and non-toxic way** was a motivating factor for our decision to invest heavily in culture formation by the end of our first year.

Upholding company values: staying resolute in the face of defection

It was just after our one-year anniversary, I was about six months pregnant, and while we felt some breathing room, nothing had been easy leading up to this point. One manager in particular had a strong grip on our team, but not in a good way. Distrust and discontent had spread quickly throughout the production floor, and it was clear that this manager was the source of the problem. She complained to her team about her recent pay increase, arguing that she deserved more for gaining the trust of a new and large client. Her large team quickly adopted her view. One day, I called her into the office and reiterated my American, meritocratic, and egalitarian leadership style. I told her that I was open to discussing compensation, but she needed to help me understand why she deserved more. I gave her a self-assessment form and said we could discuss in a few days. She took offense and promptly told her team she was leaving to start her own competing business. What she didn't tell them was that her U.S. visa had come through, and she was leaving in a few months anyway. Two weeks later, her team started resigning, citing a whole array of reasons. Some even tried to sabotage the company and brought a labor case against me. However, the core team and I remained committed to our values, and the defectors found it difficult to maintain an upper hand in the narrative. Everyone knew they had violated ethics by taking confidential information, but we remained resolute in our values and kept the faith that the truth would prevail. And it did.

Always looking ahead

Becoming a successful entrepreneur requires a unique combination of skills, strategies, and mindset. Establishing a strong work routine, using co-working spaces, prioritizing exercise, and celebrating early wins can help overcome the challenges of starting a business. At the core of all of these strategies is a willingness to take risks, be flexible, and embrace learning from experience. Whether you're just starting out or have been in business for years, remember that entrepreneurship is a journey, and each step you take is an opportunity to learn and grow.

Above all, remain focused on what motivates you. Starting a business for what it affords you beyond money means that you are motivated by more than just the financial rewards that come with being an entrepreneur. While money is certainly a crucial factor in any business venture, it should not be the sole driving force behind your decision to start a business. A study conducted by researchers at Purdue

University found that happiness increased with income, but only up to a certain point (and not as high as you'd think). Beyond that point, there was no significant increase in happiness with increasing income.

Remain cognizant of that important threshold, and find your motivation in the freedom and flexibility that owning your own business can provide. Starting a business can offer you the opportunity to control your own schedule, make your own decisions, and pursue your passions on your own terms. It can also give you the chance to make a positive impact on your community or society as a whole. When you prioritize freedom over money, you are more likely to make choices that align with your values and allow you to live a fulfilling and meaningful life, deepening the integrity of your leadership and your organization. So, if you're considering starting a business, it's important to ask yourself why you want to do it and what you hope to gain from it. If the answer is simply money, you may want to reconsider your motivations and explore other paths to financial success. But if you're motivated by the desire for freedom and the opportunity to make a positive impact, then entrepreneurship might just be the perfect path for you.

Laurice Chiongbian

Qavalo, Inc.

Helping the World Rebuild a Healthcare Workforce for the Future

Qavalo was established in 2016 by President and CEO Laurice Chiongbian, a communications expert from California and a strong advocate of entrepreneurship in the Philippines. Qavalo is a Cebu-based healthcare business process outsourcing company offering integrated clinical staffing solutions and back-office support to home health agencies in the United States.

After 12 years of work and leadership experience in Asia, Chiongbian built Qavalo upon seeing the growing challenges in the home health landscape in the U.S. with the rapid globalization of healthcare through technology. Qavalo invests in a skilled workforce of healthcare professionals in the Philippines to support the changing needs of US home health providers who are challenged with delivering quality patient care in the face of a declining clinical labor force, thereby creating the perfect synergy of supply and demand.

As the chief strategist and leadership coach of Qavalo, Chiongbian has been piloting Qavalo's overall operations while nurturing a culture of wellness, driven by her vision of realizing quality of life through providing quality healthcare. Since the company's founding, it has always been Chiongbian's mission to create meaningful and innovative career opportunities for those in healthcare. This includes cultivating a progressive, values-driven workplace where everyone feels safe, valued, and happy. As a result, these initiatives have been recognized through various business awards, with Qavalo rightfully earning the badge of a great workplace.

Building Tech-enabled Solutions for Sustainable Home Healthcare

Under the leadership of Chiongbian and her forward-thinking approach to pursuing technological innovations, Qavalo has evolved from being a traditional outsourcing provider into a progressive and data-driven business partner. Over the years, Qavalo has quickly differentiated by integrating innovations in business workflows with projects that have harnessed the powers of automation, data synchronization, and data intelligence, resulting in game-changing solutions for clients and internal operations alike.

With continuous innovation, Qavalo has maintained its position as the largest tech-enabled home health business process outsourcing in Asia, with a team of nearly 100 healthcare professionals. "In the coming years, we expect that our ongoing projects in data science applications and augmented clinical technology will drive the future of Qavalo, if not the U.S. home health industry as a whole," said Chiongbian in a statement during the company's fifth anniversary celebration.

Looking to the future, Chiongbian is committed to further innovations and expanding Qavalo's service offerings in response to industry demands and the evolving healthcare landscape.

www.Qavalo.com
https://www.linkedin.com/company/qavalo
https://www.linkedin.com/in/lauricechiongbian

Mawi Fojas de Ocampo

Living Mindfully as the Path to Our Purpose

The road to my purpose has been a bumpy ride, full of challenges, disappointments, disasters, and loss. On the parallel side of these difficulties are revelations, lessons learned, and the building of resilience. When faced with unbearable adversity and pain, I turn to the advice of a dear and wise childhood friend, "You will be surprised at how strong you are."

I'm a strong believer that finding our purpose commences with living intentionally, and living intentionally starts with self-awareness. Self-awareness begins with knowing yourself on a deeper level, and really knowing and understanding what your values are. Never underestimate the power of your passions to propel you towards knowing your values, which will then lead you to your purpose.

I understand this is not at all as simple as it may sound. Speaking for myself, it has been a decades-long, complex, and arduous process and journey, many times frustrating and debilitating. In fact, it all began with chaos.

THE FOUR Cs: Chaos, Clarity, Calm, Creation

Chaos

A working mom for more than 20 years now, I have suffered what many moms like me have: guilt about never being a good enough mom and wife and the perennial balancing act of longing to be both the best mother while struggling to perform at my peak in the workplace. This constant tug of war has caused much emotional and mental turmoil. When I am at work, I feel guilty about not being at home with my family who needs me, and when I am at home, I feel inadequate about not working hard enough to deliver the results that my employer needs.

Along the way, tragedies have taken place — a financial crisis from losing our jobs that led to losing our home, health emergencies resulting in further financial burdens all while striving to pay for tuition fees and rent. On top of this, being the primary caregiver to my aging ailing father and ultimately suffering the sudden unexpected loss of my mother. Multi-tasking became the unreasonable and almost impossible norm. Managing demanding work responsibilities, fulfilling various family commitments, taking care of our rambunctious toddler Yorkie. I cried desperately to myself, "It is all too much for one person to handle!" On multiple occasions, I felt like I would explode and have a meltdown. My body longed for rest, so much so that I seriously considered checking myself into the hospital just to have one week's worth of uninterrupted sleep, relishing the thought of being hooked up to an IV line that could feed me intravenously so that I wouldn't have to get up to eat.

Exhausted from so much giving, I declared how much I hated my life and longed to disappear, even wishing to just die already so that I could finally rest and have some peace.

Clarity

I questioned why "bad things" were "happening to me" and resented God. This resentment brewed into anger, and during fits of exasperation, I even affirmed how much I hated God for "allowing" such events.

And yet, through this treacherous journey called life, I began to wake up and come into my purpose. Slowly, the insights began to unfurl, layer by layer. Eventually, I learned and realized that these challenges, difficulties, obstacles, disasters, and tragedies were here to:

1. Offer a point of comparison, allowing me to see and appreciate the blessings that I DO have, helping me develop a mindset of gratitude, ultimately teaching me how to expand these gifts in my life.
2. Show me what I DON'T want.
3. Remind me of my divine power to manifest the life that I DO want.
4. Prepare me for what I have been asking for all along.

5. Help me grow and transform into the being I am truly meant to be – my authentic self.
6. Develop compassion for others as I move towards this calling of service.

I learned that thoughts are just that – thoughts or reactions which are ruled by fear and impulse and are not necessarily true and lasting versus intentional and meaningful responses which are ruled by truth. My passion as a seeker grew, and ironically, it was chaos that fanned these flames of desire for self-awareness. From this space of self-discovery, my values became clear: to live mindfully and intentionally, to heed the call of service, to honor my authentic self. It is proof that chaos IS the way. Chaos IS the path. There is no other way out of the mayhem and madness except to go *through* it. And the heartbreak of this process may have been necessary to do just that--break open my heart to create the space I needed to welcome in self-love where I would meet my authentic self.

From this space of self-discovery, my values became clear: to live mindfully and intentionally, to heed the call of service, to honor my authentic self.

Calm

As I allowed the authentic self to emerge, a sense of peace and calm washed over my being. Through the practice of Momentism as taught to me by my guru, Salliji, I stepped into the empowered space of the present moment. Bowing deeply to the lessons of the past with reverence, understanding and appreciating their lessons, while looking up and out to the future with a welcoming heart open to what's in store, free of fear, uncertainty, and anxiety – basking in the beauty and power of the present moment, just *being* rather than *doing*.

Creation

This new empowered space of mindful and intentional living in the present moment birthed courageous and conscious creation. A new belief system emerged from within – that I can build a sustainable and financially secure life while living my soul purpose. This mindset shift propelled me towards my dream of returning to my work as an editor and writer, building my practice as a bamboo wand and slow movement meditation teacher, and carrying out my role as a grief counselor.

As an editor and writer, my personal values are to inspire and educate because in so doing, we also empower and enable. I believe that at the heart of editorial work is service, and I feel grateful for this privilege to return to my first love to honor my divine purpose and soul mission. As writers, we have the unique opportunity to transform minds and hearts, create culture change, and spark the desire in others to do the same and make a difference.

I founded Yu Hezu Bamboo Wand and Slow Movement Meditation in 2015 after learning the art of the bamboo wand from Salliji in 2008. It is based on an ancient Chinese practice originally devised for the royal family of China which was kept secret for thousands of years.

Motion meditation best describes the bamboo wand practice's slow and purposeful movements derived by observing animals at play, such as "Stretching the Crane," "Twitching the Dragon's Tail," "Peeling the Octopus," "Horse's Stance on a Tightrope," and "The Tiger Springs" among others. The 17 gentle, low-impact, and deliberate movements include stretching, twisting, lunging, and bending using a light four-foot bamboo wand that moves every muscle in the body, promoting efficient blood circulation, slowing down the aging process, and prolonging life.

I first met Salliji when I was six years old as she was my parents' yoga, meditation, and breathwork teacher. She taught my dad and his fellow pilots how to combat the stress of flying. My dad sums it up, "Every time I go to work, 300 lives depend on my mental and emotional well-being." He took his responsibility as a pilot seriously and practiced mindfulness and Momentism – the art of being fully present in the moment, in the here and now, through meditating, breathing, and yoga as taught by Salliji.

In 2008, Salliji returned to Manila after decades of advocating "global spiritualization for peace" as her soul mission. Since she left the Philippines decades back to pursue a life of service, her practice expanded with a clientele ranging from ordinary citizens like my family to Hollywood celebrities like Elizabeth Taylor and Michael Caine. She has authored the book *Cosmic Arrangement*, and she was well into her eighties during this reunion with our family when she taught us the art of the bamboo wand. At the beginning, I practiced the art for personal well-being. I discovered with amazement that my back aches from scoliosis began to disappear and the quality of my sleep greatly improved. As I felt healthier and happier from the benefits I experienced from the bamboo wand, I started sharing it with family and friends. The practice has grown, and companies have requested bamboo wand classes for their employees as a means to address burnout, stress, and anxiety. I am grateful for the opportunity to share the gift of the bamboo wand through workshops and well-being retreats that have taken place in Metro Manila, Tagaytay, Batangas, Puerto Galera, Palawan, and online across Asia, the United States, and Europe.

Through the last eight years of teaching the art of the bamboo wand, I have also merged the practice with the slow purposeful movements of Chi Kung. The result has been a modified version of the practice where I intuitively created 17 movements based on the bamboo wand but without the need of the wand. This version is perfect for those who may not have a bamboo wand or for those looking for their bamboo wand practice to evolve.

The Gift of Grief

During the pandemic, most of us experienced tragedy and loss, and if not directly, we witnessed friends and family who did. This devastation of loss came in all forms – losing what we deemed as a normal and familiar way of life; financially, through the loss of our jobs or businesses; and the most profound loss of all, the death of our loved ones. Such devastation we were experiencing collectively and individually compelled me to walk towards my new path of service, that of a grief counselor.

It was an enlightening journey inadvertently merging my learnings as a corporate communications professional, writer, and bamboo wand teacher. I developed the Nurturing a Grieving Heart Workshop, which I offered to those in need through a series of three online modules over the course of three months.

The first module during month one includes three main elements: Intention Setting, Self-Awareness, and Embodiment. It takes students through discussions on bereavement, grief, and mourning as well as the impact of grief on our physical, emotional, mental, and spiritual health, including the importance of self-care and rest during the grief journey. It also elaborates on the different kinds of grief as well as the six stages of grief and how these stages are never linear and may vary from one individual to another. This module ultimately offers insights into how grieving becomes our path to healing and wholeness.

During month two, the second module tackles the importance and relevance of complicated and unresolved grief through journaling and gentle embodiment as well as the healing power of forgiveness. A portion of this module focuses on the importance of practicing Momentism through the Chinese bamboo wand art and slow movement meditation.

The third module that happens on month three involves the elements of Reflection and Expression through journaling and art therapy, merged with gentle embodiment and releasing of stagnant energy through the movement practice of Thai bamboo wand. Similar to the Chinese bamboo wand, the Thai practice uses a bamboo wand, but its movements are more active and high-impact, compared to the slow, gentle movements of the Chinese art. The Thai movements may be described as active "exercises" while the Chinese practice can be referred to as gentle "innercises."

The Nurturing a Grieving Heart Workshop advocates that grief is a normal experience in our existence as humans, coming from a profound loss. It is not something to get over, but rather, it is a journey to be deeply felt and experienced in its full raw and ugly state, teaching us the gift of grief, for we only grieve as much as we have loved.

To Be Gloriously Human

Another fruit of courageous creation manifested through my participation in Buhay Retreat's Release, Rest, Renew Workshop, in collaboration with the retreat founder, Tina Baron, and my sister, Tet Fojas Bachmann. The four-day retreat took participants through a heart opening process of self-awareness and intention setting, courageously releasing and meeting our hearts. We learned how to be one with ourselves, connecting with that oneness, and honoring our true selves by practicing the art of Momentism through slow movement meditation and the art of the Chinese and Thai bamboo wand.

We acknowledged that we must first do our inner work by peeling the layers slowly, gently, so that we may become honest with ourselves and acknowledge what we would like to release, knowing that we may only release what we have brought awareness to.

We dove deep into opening ourselves to love. We activated our heart chakra, allowing rather than surrendering, and through self-awareness began to release what we want to let go of, making space for self-care, self-love, and self-nurturing. Without judgment, guilt, or shame, we basked in loving ourselves first so that we may better love and care for others. We acknowledged our shadow, knowing it is through the darkest parts of ourselves that we may find our light. We remembered that allowing our shadow to bring forth dark thoughts is okay because our

"We acknowledged our shadow, knowing it is through the darkest parts of ourselves that we may find our light. We remembered that allowing our shadow to bring forth dark thoughts is okay because our thoughts don't define who we are and our emotions don't define who we are.

thoughts don't define who we are and our emotions don't define who we are. We learned that it is from allowing the darkness of our thoughts to come forward that we may find the light from within because what we resist will persist and what we repress and suppress will fight its way to the surface.

We accepted that we are both yin and yang, light and dark, sadness and joy, fear and love. It is by allowing the most loving part of ourselves to take care of this darkest side of us the way a mother would nurture her young child, embracing her crying, defiant toddler and allowing the loving light from heart to offer soothe and calm. This is what it means to truly love all parts of ourselves and honor our authentic and true beings. It means truly believing that there is nothing wrong with us. There is nothing to be fixed and nothing to be ashamed of. When we learn to nurture, see, and listen to our shadow side, the darkness will transform into the various forms of light: patience and loving kindness. This is where we experience how it feels to be beautiful and glorious humans.

From Chaos to Courageous and Conscious Creation

The path to purpose isn't linear. Neither is it easy nor comfortable. While I offered a guide through the 4 Cs based on my own personal experience, the road is different for each and every one of us. And just when you finally feel you have made some progress and headway, the road may suddenly wind up and down and take you back to square one where you may feel utterly hopeless. It may seem like a never ending dance of two steps forward, one step back. You may feel incredibly frustrated to the point of giving up. That is okay. It is all part of the adventure called life.

Living mindfully and with intention is a powerful path to our purpose by embracing the chaos, cultivating self-awareness, developing clarity, practicing Momentism and calmness, as well as courageous and conscious creation. Never underestimate the power of your dreams. We will experience loss and tragedy, and yet, we may also embody strength and resilience, building courage and compassion while helping others along the way. It is a constant inner journey of manifesting a life that is meaningful, joyful, and fulfilling even *amidst* challenges, difficulties, tragedies, and crises, because you are in full alignment with your deepest values, passions, soul mission, and divine purpose while honoring your highest, most authentic self.

Mawi Fojas de Ocampo

A working mom for 23 years, Mawi Fojas de Ocampo's experience encompasses corporate communications, brand building, reputation management, internal and external communications, digital marketing, social media management, content creation, events management, public relations, media relations, and crisis management – spanning the industries of lifestyle media and publishing, real estate, healthcare, banking, hospitality, and the performance arts. Mawi is currently the managing editor of the Philippines' longest running lifestyle and society magazine. Her other roles are writer, bamboo wand and slow movement meditation teacher, and certified grief counselor. She received her certification from the American Academy of Grief Counseling under the American Institute of Healthcare Professionals. She lives in Manila and is mom to three children, ages 27, 24, and 23. Also, she is grandmom to their yorkie, Frenkie. Mawi dreams of living by the sea as a full-time beach bum while writing her novel one day.

Instagram: @livemindfullyph
https://www.instagram.com/livemindfullyph/
LinkedIn: Maritess (Mawi) Fojas de Ocampo

Nica Jones

SCULPTED BY STRUGGLES

I- The Shaping of my Youth

I was born into a clan of simple but matriarchal personas who set possibilities before my feet.

I remember my grandmother as a hardworking woman. She persevered in life although she was uneducated and a widow after she gave birth to her ninth and last child. By the time she retired, she owned one income-earning property, a fully paid home, and access to money that she loaned to people for additional income. My mom, like her mother, also lacked education, but was a serial entrepreneur. There is nothing in my youth that ever suggested that I couldn't achieve anything as a girl.

The youngest of five siblings and the only girl, I grew up boyish and enjoyed the games played by my brothers. I was ambulant to the girly toys my mom gave me. By the time I hit 13 years old, I was amazed how my body suddenly changed. The change in my hormones made me look more like a young woman than a girl. At this stage, people started to look at me differently.

I remember one instance when my school bus driver said to me, "*You will never amount to anything because you will get pregnant by high school.*" I smile at this memory because in hindsight, he almost got it right. I did get pregnant early in college, but I always knew that I was worth something. Some people come into your life and plant a seed of doubt in your mind. Then one day, you will come to realize that you have been living with it all along – a kind of mental fog in the background of your mind.

While still in my youth, my mother would already send me to pay income taxes and do other adult tasks. This is where I learned to grow up fast and to talk to elders in a serious fashion. Upon reflection, such years of training prepared me for my future growth and sturdied my grit.

During high school, I was a consistent honor student, and I graduated salutatorian of my class. Loving athletics through which I gained confidence, I played volleyball and excelled in several extracurricular activities. Life was bustling, busy, and exciting.

II- Here Comes the Lemons

My father became an overseas worker when I was two years old. He was a good man, a good provider, and generous to all his family and friends. For the 20 years that he worked in Saudi Arabia, he would spend only 45 days with us once a year. I always looked forward to these visits as he showered me with gold necklaces and other jewelry. His generosity was boundless to his other family members and friends, but it had its drawbacks. Unfortunately during these good times, he and my mom failed to save for the future. After 20 years, the "party train" stopped, and the pantry became bare. They didn't have the savings to maintain a reasonable lifestyle. On top of that, my father became ill.

Trying to get away from the money troubles at home, I ended up getting pregnant. I married a younger man who did not have ambition. He was raised by very loving and enabling parents. In 1999, I gave birth to twin boys. I grew up instantly upon laying my eyes on them. I made a solemn vow that I would do my best to provide the best life that I could to my sons, Zach and Zeth.

To have them when I was 21 years old was not easy. My husband Junjun was almost four years younger than me. We lived with his family, and they were very good to us. I had such deep love for my mother- and father-in-law, and they loved us right back. I worked several jobs within their family business – greeter, cashier, and waitress. I even tutored my husband's younger siblings.

One day, I came home from a hard day of work to my husband and kids. I was excited to see them. It was dark in the house, and as soon as I entered the house, I saw Junjun lying down on the couch. He then jumped up and attacked me. He sucker punched me, pulled my hair, threatened me with a knife, banged my head on the wall, and bit my nose until it bled. In short, he gave me a beat down.

Though we had had verbal arguments before, he had never physically attacked me. It all came as a surprise. This was also the first time he ever laid his hands on me in the four years that we were together. When he recognized the magnitude of his actions, he ordered me to get in the car with my sons. To my surprise, he rushed us into the car and drove me and the kids to his parent's place. At his parents' house, I called my mom to ask for help. They arrived in two hours' time and ordered me to come with them. By then, I was experiencing Stockholm syndrome. I didn't want to leave anymore. My father, seeing my beaten face, said to me in a tone that shuddered through me, "If you do not come with us, you can never call for help anymore." And so I went with them.

Two weeks later, my husband left for Davao, which is a southern province far from Metro Manila. I remember that it was Mother's Day of 2003 when I learned of his departure. I wanted to pack my bags and leave everything behind just so I could be with him. His mom asked me to give Junjun time to heal, and so again, I did.

While in Manila, I applied for a call center job and was accepted. My first day at work, I called Junjun to share my excitement for this job. I also looked forward to seeing him and told him that the twins missed him already. He apologized for the pain that he had caused and said that he was ready to come back home. There was a sign of relief in the air. I started my work at 8:00 a.m. that day, and it ended at about 3:00 p.m. I called him as I was about to ride the shuttle, but his phone just rang. I tried several times to call him that evening until his phone no longer rang. Apprehension lingered in the air.

At about 5:00 a.m. the next day, I got a message on my phone asking what my relationship was to the person who owned that number. With apprehension and confusion, I said, "I am his wife." Then a guy called me from the police station and delivered the bad news to me. Junjun was dead. He was in an altercation about 4:00 p.m. the day before and was shot dead. At 26 years of age, I was officially a widow.

III- Tragedies Continue

Out of money, my parents sold their house to have money for living expenses. The loss of dignity permanently marked them. The proceeds of an investment they had made to a security agency brought some relief. Less than two years after they made the investment, an acquisition occurred. Since the investment was "off the books," my parents' investment was not recognized. Short story, they lost most of their money.

During this period, my dad was also diagnosed with stage 4 bone cancer. By December 2004, I had to turn the life support off my father. We didn't have the money to get him into the ICU. To this day, it was one of the most difficult things I ever had to do.

If that was not enough, another tragedy struck.

In 2005, my father-in-law surrendered to depression. No more than 20 minutes after arriving home from work, I heard two loud bangs that startled me. Rushing to his side, I found him lying in a pool of blood, lifeless. I stood in shock as the scene swirled around me.

He was the man who expressed support to me and the kids after my husband died. He told everyone that we were to remain part of their family. Now that help and support were in jeopardy; that premonition came true. That same year, this family that I loved dearly kicked me out. There had been rumors, stirred by others, that I had had an affair with my father-in-law. It never happened. Period. To this day, it hurt that my good relationship with him was tarnished with malice.

IV- Talking Straight with God

While all these things were happening from 2003-2007, I found solace in my work. I was promoted seven times as I channeled all my pain and sorrow into grit. Though I was getting consistent salary increases,

I also messed up my finances as my relationship with money hovered like "a one-day millionaire," as we say in the Philippines.

By the end of 2007, I decided that I would shore up my life. I had my kids relying on me to be a responsible parent. I had to shape up, and so I did. I racked up a credit card bill of about P40k. I then took out a loan from a bank so I could pay my credit card bill. With focus, determination, and consistency, I was out of debt after 18 months.

I started to feel happy in 2007. It felt like my life was okay, and I had breathing room. I enjoyed a good balance of work, time with my kids, and sports. I didn't have savings, but it was a far cry from feeling the crushing weight of debt.

At night, I would utter a small prayer from the deepest part of my heart. It went like this: *"Lord, if you will send someone my way, please make it a foreigner."* Why not a Filipino? I already had two kids. Back then, I thought that a foreigner would love me plus two kids easier than a Filipino would. I thought it would be less complicated.

In 2008, I met and dated an Italian diplomat. I thought my prayer had been answered. But not until the endless Elvis Presley songs and topics I could not generationally connect with did I realize that he was not "The One."

I then went back to the drawing board with God. They say that when you pray, be specific. So then I specifically asked, *"Lord, I probably wasn't clear about many things other than a foreigner. If you can kindly grant me a good-looking man, smart, and kind between the ages of 45-50, then I would truly appreciate that."* One month after my revised prayer, I met my future husband, Keith. He would also be one of the most instrumental persons to shape who I'd become and my relationship with money.

Remember all the tragedies that happened to me? I just couldn't articulate it, but I recognized the lessons learned. I needed to be a responsible mama and give my kids better opportunities in life. That was the beginning of the turnaround of my finances.

V- Deliberate Focus Pays Off

Everything in my life became deliberate when I found my traction with savings. I had come to realize that the life lessons I already learned were fuel to take life head-on. Remember the part where I was good with work? Oh yes, I love performance management. I was and still am a visual person, and I saw problems from that view. I got excited to overcome challenges in creative and fun ways. I wrote down all the problems in front of me and tackled them head-on. The first challenge was to create an emergency fund. Twelve months later, I secured my first substantial emergency fund. I was now in total control.

With the rise of Facebook, I developed my community of friends and family. They saw my success and wanted to tap into my "secrets." With everything I had gone through, I felt humbled, and I thought that by giving some of my old colleagues' financial assistance and guidance, I could help them. But I thought that I would do it with a twist. Not only would they get the assistance they needed, but I would also teach them the "secrets" of financial wellness. I wanted my friends to feel like they were my family, not just Facebook friends. I provided them a safe place to borrow money, accommodated them even during unholy hours as most outsourcing employees work graveyard shifts. I was making an impact on their lives. By listening closely to their pains, my empathy deepened. Their experiences and hardships were powerful reminders that I should stay humble.

My greatest weapons were my life challenges. And though now older than my co-workers, my resilience, passion, and hunger shone through as examples to them and my sons.

Borne out of all these challenges emerged Global CreditPros. It is the company that represents my values and the mission to give Filipinos a fighting chance to a life with dignity upon retirement. My company's vision is to get Filipinos out of the cycle of debt and onto a path of retirement.

VI- Breaking Generational Curses

If my life was a video game, it surely didn't start at the easiest level. Giving birth to twins at 21, losing my husband at 26, then my dad dying in my hands must be a stage in the game where you have to take down the Boss Enemy in order to survive. The tragic suicide of my father-in-law and the subsequent loss of security and financial well-being for my children coupled with the need to care for my mother surely placed me at the Advanced level of the game called Life.

While back then these events seemed to be all tragedies, they were actually my training ground for strength, creativity, determination, humor, resilience, and empathy. I look back as I tell these stories, and I am thankful that it happened in my youth.

"While back then these events seemed to be all tragedies, they were actually my training ground for strength, creativity, determination, humor, resilience, and empathy. I look back as I tell these stories, and I am thankful that it happened in my youth.

My advocacy of financial wellness spread. One close friend referred another, and another, and another, until it spread like wildfire. The cascading impact of Global CreditPros resulted in hundreds of videos and testimonies chronicling how we touched lives. The result was a library of authentic stories from clients that then evolved to a program that we call "Real Stories, Real Solutions." I trained thousands of souls in person, via webinars, and with personalized one-on-one coaching. My joy was in listening to them as their stories resonated with my soul. Talking to each one of our clients became a way of life. They would talk not only of money issues but would share family stories as well.

That's when that lightbulb moment happened for me.

Their stories are no different than mine. The scenarios may have some differences, but the gist of the stories was almost the same. They were trapped in a sandwich generation. Most of the parents of the people I helped out did not prepare for retirement. I saw that one day, they would be asked to decide between life and money, an experience no different from the experience I had had with my dad. To lose dignity at the end of their lives. I just could not bear that.

This is when I realized that my life from early on had been designed to teach me the skills that could help change people's lives for the better by teaching them a path to financial wellness. I realized the technical skills I learned from my corporate stint, though essential, were not sufficient. The years of hardships taught me a level of empathy that would go beyond just me and be embodied by those who represent Global CreditPros.

What was supposed to be a small venture to replace my income turned out to be one of the biggest avenues to execute all the lessons I had learned in life.

Global CreditPros allowed me to feed my entrepreneurial spirit while simultaneously changing people's lives.

VII- Not Being a Prisoner of the Past

My soul is old, but my spirit is young and vibrant. My persona adapted with today's ways in more ways that I can imagine. As an insecure person who doubted myself at every step of the way, I'm surprised I got this far. I know that even as I have prospered well, I am traumatized by my past and carry weights in life I shouldn't have.

When I turned 45 less than a year ago and from the time I wrote this story, I had a change of heart. I have been trying to work from the background, not wanting to fully spread my wings. Finally at 45, I have accepted that my life was never just meant for me. That all the pains from the past were meant as stepping stones for me to find my own power, my own fulfillment, and to touch others.

My financial wellness talks are a combination of hard and soft skills, done in an ultra-dramatic but humorous way.

VIII- Forward-Bound: The Journey Ahead

My past was a beautiful, exciting, and dramatic obstacle course. I look back and realize that amidst the tragedies, I had a great time with my life. I dated some interesting men, had fun adventures with friends, and tremendously enjoyed raising the twins. Facing the challenges of raising twins will never compare to the love my sons brought to my life. They brought meaning to my existence. My husband Keith, who shared the same passion to help others, inspired me and empowered me to always move forward.

So forward I go.

Today, my life is a fine balance of sports, wellness, work, family, travel, mentoring people on how to get out of debt, and just having a good time. My expertise on budgeting got so good that I budget even my caloric intake.

I believe in a world where everyone has a chance for a good life. A chance to secure a life of quality, especially upon retirement, so that we don't have to be a burden to our families. No person should ever have to be stressed by the financial part of taking care of their parents nor any child should ever have to choose between life or death of a parent.

"I believe in a world where everyone has a chance for a good life. A chance to secure a life of quality, especially upon retirement, so that we don't have to be a burden to our families. No person should ever have to be stressed by the financial part of taking care of their parents nor any child should ever have to choose between life or death of a parent.

I will work hard to give each one a fighting chance to complete this journey of life with dignity.

My advocacy for financial wellness through discipline on budget and getting the entire household to be part of the strategy is my passion.

Recently, I received a confirmation that after working with my one of my personal mentees for two years, that he is officially out of debt and has secured four months of emergency funds.

I am officially part of lives changed for the better, slowly fulfilling my mission, and this chapter has only begun!

The level of excitement is crazy!

My life is far from perfect. It's just that these imperfections are just so perfect for me!

Nica Jones

Nica is in the business of changing people's lives for the better through financial wellness. She started her early life with a common Filipino story. A breadwinner.

She piloted a project of providing access to credit that promoted understanding of money and that eventually was the beginning of CreditPros, a company in the business of disrupting the cycle of debt and taking Filipinos onto a path of retirement.

Since 2017, Nica and her CreditPros team have grown the business over 1000%, achieved profitability in year 3 and trained over 2000 people on financial wellness while maintaining top-tier customer experience centered in empathy, resulting in a library of videos and picture from clients, debuted as Real Stories, Real Solutions.

Before GCP, Nica was part of the BPO workforce from 2003 to 2011. She started as a customer sales agent, promoted seven times in five years. This was about the same time she faced major life challenges.

She moved on as a client services manager of an architectural firm with focus in Asia and the U.S. This experience eventually led her to the maritime industry, impacting training, client services, and sales often exceeding company targets.

Her life is a fine balance of health, serving the community, and loving her family.

Her story may have started the same as most Filipinos, but her ending is anything but sad.

Years of perseverance, discipline, humor, resilience, and commitment is now not only being received by her family but her small-kind-of-big world as well.

Nica Jones
nica@globalcreditpros.com
https://www.linkedin.com/in/ronica-pineda-jones-2b788b15

Monica V. Maralit

Finding Purpose in the Unexpected Path of Life

Most young people may have a general, rough idea of what they want to do when they grow up, or they may not know what they really want to do. At different points in my life, I really felt like I knew what I wanted to do. I knew what I wanted to be and spend my life doing. I was convinced that everything would work out. It was very clear although life is never that predictable and rarely happens the way we plan. My career story takes a journey over several decades and different countries.

At different points in my life, I really felt like I knew what I wanted to do. I knew what I wanted to be and spend my life doing. I was convinced that everything would work out. It was very clear although life is never that predictable and rarely happens the way we plan.

Singapore

One December, for the Christmas holiday, I was in Singapore with my family. My 25-year-old nephew asked me, "Tita Monica, when you were my age or younger did you always know what you wanted to do? Did you always know what you wanted to be?" I proceeded to tell him my career story. I said, growing up, I wanted to be a doctor. Because my parents were all in the medical field, that was what I was exposed to. Thus, when I was young, I wanted to be a doctor. A pediatrician, then an OB-GYN, then a neonatal cardiothoracic surgeon. Yes, I was an ambitious child. I wanted to not only be a surgeon for newborn babies, but a surgeon that fixed their little baby hearts. At this point, I had not realized that I don't do well with blood or open flesh.

Becoming a Neonatal Cardiothoracic Surgeon
Florida, USA

As my parents always made sure that we saw them work so that we understood the value of work and where money came from, when I was around 11 years old, while living in a small town in north Florida, my stepfather who is a surgeon took me to watch one of his surgeries. A girl my age needed an emergency appendectomy. At the hospital, the nurses took me in, dressed me in too-big scrubs, put a scrub cap on my head that almost covered my eyes, and taught me how to scrub in like a doctor. When they brought me into the surgical room, I stood on a foot stool at the patient's head to watch. The girl's belly had been prepped for the surgery, sterilized, and taped off. The anesthesiologist showed me his anesthesia machine and all its buttons, knobs, and monitors beeping and blipping. They all called me Dr. Monica. I felt very important.

As if I were in medical school in my first live surgery class, my stepfather proceeded to explain what was going to happen next. "I'm going to take this scalpel and cut through the epidermis, then the dermis, then the subcutaneous fatty layer, then the facia, then the muscle, then we'll find the large intestine, and the appendix will be at the end of the large intestine. We'll snip it off, sew it up, suture, suture, suture. Done!" Great! Easy! I'm excited and ready!

He made his first clean cut beside the patient's belly button and I could see blood flow, the open flesh, and presumably, the subcutaneous fatty layer. I could feel the blood draining from my face and head, and I became light-headed. I stumbled backward, and a nurse and the anesthesiologist caught me as everything turned dark. After what seemed like an hour, but was only about 30 seconds, I woke up and found myself sitting in a chair, still at the head of the patient, and everyone looking at me. I was mortified. The nurse looked at me over the top of her glasses and asked very seriously, eyebrow raised, "Dr. Monica, are you ready?" I sheepishly nodded and my stepfather proceeded – subcutaneous fatty layer, facia, muscle, large intestine, appendix, snip, sew, suture, suture, suture. Done!

My stepfather explained that the patient was going to rest at the hospital for a day or two. Then, after a few weeks, the stitches would come out and she would be fine and healthy again. He said that if her appendix had ruptured her situation might've been life-threatening. The nurse turned to me and said, again very seriously, "Congratulations. We saved a life today, Dr. Monica." This was probably my first glimpse into wanting to be a surgeon and wanting to help others at a deeper level, literally and figuratively. At 11 years old, I knew exactly what I wanted to do, with conviction. Neonatal cardiothoracic surgeon.

Becoming an Inspiring Talk Show Host
Bangkok, Thailand

When high school came around, we moved to Bangkok, Thailand. In the early 1990s, Thailand was still not very exposed to Western culture, and not a lot of people spoke English. TV shows and movies in English were very few. When I first moved there, I remember only two American shows on TV, "MacGyver" and "Solid Gold," and both were dubbed in Thai. To watch in English, I had to listen to the English recording on the radio and mute my TV. Eventually, more and more American influences started to seep in through the influx of expatriates. Along with that, we got the U.S. version of CNN and, for some reason, Oprah. I was mesmerized and taken by Oprah. She had different guests on her show who would tell their stories; some were heartbreaking, and some were not. Oprah always seemed to get people to a realization point that they were better than they thought they were, that they deserved happiness, and that they could attain happiness if they just made the decision to do this or that. Oprah helped people realize their purpose, rewarded those who helped others, and just encouraged people to go out and live their best lives as a steward of strength to themselves and to others. Thus, I wanted to do that too. I wanted to be Oprah. A proud, strong Black woman ready to help others realize their best selves. So, I studied her career path as a journalist and talk show host. I watched Oprah every day and jotted down every question she asked to understand the guests' backstories and motivations. I wrote down her leading questions that brought about an eventual epiphany and self-realization for her guests. I would watch these shows and take down notes, and then write an article about that same show. I thought this was a great way to practice my journalistic writing skills. I even practiced interviewing imaginary guests in the privacy of my bedroom. After every interview, my imaginary guests realized their full potential and thanked me profusely for changing their lives. At 16 years old, I knew exactly what I wanted to do: abandon my pursuit of being a neonatal cardiothoracic surgeon and become Asian Oprah.

Becoming an International Broadcast Journalist
Manila, Philippines

After graduating from high school, I moved to Manila, Philippines. I enrolled in Ateneo de Manila University and majored in Communication Arts with the intent to focus on broadcast journalism. I was extremely excited and felt that I had found a home and purpose for my future as a journalist. All of my classes were fun, interesting, and aligned to my goal and more. I learned about TV and radio broadcasting, advertising, and marketing. I was already practicing my closing line for CNN, hairbrush in hand like a mic, standing in front of my bathroom mirror, "I'm Monica Maralit in Belgrade, and ***this*** (dramatic pause) is CNN." I imagined myself to be anywhere in the world breaking an amazing story of corruption in corporate conglomerate ranks or social injustice to the people of underprivileged societies, "I'm Monica Maralit in Johannesburg, and ***this*** (dramatic pause and slight nod) is CNN." At 20 years old, I knew exactly what I wanted to do.

In my last year of college, I was doing my thesis and on-the-job training with the Philippines' leading television stations, like ABS-CBN and GMA, specifically in the news division. Again, this was in line with following Oprah's path of becoming a reporter and eventual talk show host. I was assigned to the OB vans, or outside broadcasting vans, that would follow reporters throughout the day and broadcast the news live or tape parts of the reporters' stories to be shown during the evening or late-night news. My role was basically to be the assistant to the production assistant or assist the reporters or cameramen. I would help carry cables, pin mic lapels, ensure continuity in a shot, sign in reporters or crew when we had to enter different buildings like the Senate, etc. I observed the reporters as they talked to different people to find the stories or talk to the OB crew about how they wanted their shot or editors about what to edit in their story. At first, it was very exciting and fun to see the news that evening and be able to say I was there. Though after a while, it wasn't what I thought it would be. There wasn't any cracking down and discovering corporate corruption or social injustice. There was no damaging lines of questioning to politicians to break them down. There was a lot of searching for places and people and waiting around in the heat. I also observed that reporters had to turn a blind eye to certain things in order to maintain a relationship and get a story. My interest was waning in this particular field. I still graduated with a degree in Communication Arts though my grip on my dream of being Asian Oprah was slipping.

At 22 years old, with a degree in Communication Arts, I did not know exactly what I wanted to do. I had spent much of the summer post-graduation on my couch at home watching MTV's Real World and Road Rules or on the phone with my ride-or-die friends while eating ice cream and peanut butter straight out of the jar. As this was the post-Reality Bites and pre-iPhone/Facebook/Instagram/TikTok era, our cordless analog phones at home were the lifelines of our newly responsibility-free existence. My mother was not amused. She told me that I had to get a job as she was done paying for my education, food, and shelter, and it was now time for me to be a responsible adult. She said was going to start charging me rent if I was going to continue living at home. As I did not have any means to pay that rent, I had to find a job. Fortunately, a more responsible friend was working in HR at Citibank, and he suggested that I apply to Citiphone. Thus started my career in the corporate world and specifically in contact centers. My mom wasn't happy about it, thinking that I was a telephone operator answering customer service calls. She said, "I didn't send you to private schools and university so that you could be a telephone operator. Do you think you can double your salary in five years?"

I did it in two years when I moved to eTelecare Global Solutions, one of the first Business Process Outsourcers in the country. I was the 27th employee hired. This was the dawn of the Philippine BPO industry in 2000. My career flourished, and I became a team manager, operations manager, and client manager. "In the early years, I even remember being interviewed by CNN about this new industry in the country and the reporter asked, where do you see yourself in 5 years. I pointed to the office of the president of the company." When I left the company almost 10 years later, eTelecare had over 13,000 employees and a global footprint. I continued to manage operations when I moved to a Recruiting Process Outsourcer called PSG Global Solutions. There were only 20 people in the company when I started, and 15 years later, it has over 4,000 employees and a global presence. The company supports recruiting services to some of the top global multinational companies. Now, I head the region for PSG Global Solutions and am president of Find Human Resources, PSG's local Philippine recruiting arm. "We are poised to open another division specializing in international placements of Filipino workers."

Finding my Ikigai

At this point in my career story that I was telling my nephew, he looked at me and said, "That's a great story, Tita Monica. What does that have to do with me?"

I said, "Well, to answer your question, I did know what I wanted to do when I was 11. I wanted to be a surgeon. I knew what I wanted to be when I was 16. I wanted to be Oprah. I knew what I wanted to do when I was 20. I wanted to be a journalist for CNN. But I didn't do any of those things. I found myself going down a path during a time I didn't know what I wanted. I found myself in the corporate world in the middle of thousands of people and eventually managing and developing employees. Then, I realized that I was actually doing what I wanted to do all along. I wanted to

"Then, I realized that I was actually doing what I wanted to do all along. I wanted to help others improve their lives, help them realize their best selves, and live authentic lives. It was just a different means by which I was doing it. But the purpose of my life is the same."

help others improve their lives, help them realize their best selves, and live authentic lives. It was just a different means by which I was doing it. But the purpose of my life is the same."

This brings me to purpose. I drew upon the wisdom of the Japanese and told my nephew about the concept of Ikigai. Ikigai is to live the realization of what one hopes for. It's about finding happiness, fulfillment, and balance in the regular routine of your daily life. So, I used this concept in this perspective of finding purpose in your work or finding work that has a purpose for you.

There are four questions to ask that will help you draw nearer to Ikigai.

Question 1 - What do you love?

It can be anything that makes you feel good; something that you would willingly do anytime. It's something that will get your dopamine levels up, and anytime you have the chance to talk about it and share it with others, you would gladly do so in a heartbeat. No one can stop you from talking and talking and talking about it. It can be as simple as a hobby, such as writing, creating videos, taking photos, painting, dancing, baking cakes, or counting stars. It could be a hobby, a concept, an initiative, or anything that you feel passionate about.

We've all heard that if you do what you love, then you never work a day in your life. That may be a bit of stretch, but if you do what you love, then it makes the days and weeks and months a lot more enjoyable. Though, it's not all about love.

Question 2 - What are you good at?

It's something that you excel at. It pertains to skills and competencies. People always tell you, "Hey, you're really good at this! You should do this more!" It might be something that you've always been good at as you were born with this natural skill. We all know people with whom we are amazed at how easy it is for them to pick up a skill. They can do math in their head with ease. Their hand-eye coordination is so good that they pick up sports easily. It can also be something that you've honed over years. You learned it, practiced it over and over, and now excel in it. It can be public speaking, a sport, or math. Anything that you can do effortlessly or are considered an expert at.

Question 3 - What does the world need?

It's something that the world needs or a community needs. It makes the world a better place to live. It's something that we do that contributes to a bigger whole. It contributes to bettering the world or people's lives. It may be altruistic or not. Many times, we think of this as our vision. What the world needs may be a technology that connects people during a time when we cannot be physically together. It may be a new product or service that benefits human needs. It may also be addressing social or environmental woes.

Question 4 - What can you get paid for?

Since we need to live our own lives, we need to eat, we need clothes on our backs, we need to feed our families, we need to send them to school, etc. We need to get paid. It's not enough that we love what we do. We're good at it, and the world needs it. But we need to be compensated for it because we have our daily expenses and people who depend on us. This last question really pertains to what the world is willing to pay for. If you can't get paid for the work that you do, it may bring fullness and delight, but you will not be able to pay your bills and fulfill your responsibilities. For practicality purposes, this question needs to be satisfied.

If these four questions were placed in a Venn diagram like the one below, we can see the circles representing the four questions will intersect. The intersection between two circles describes what your passion, mission, vocation, and profession may be. The intersection of all circles in the center of these is our Ikigai. Our purpose, our meaning, our reason for being.

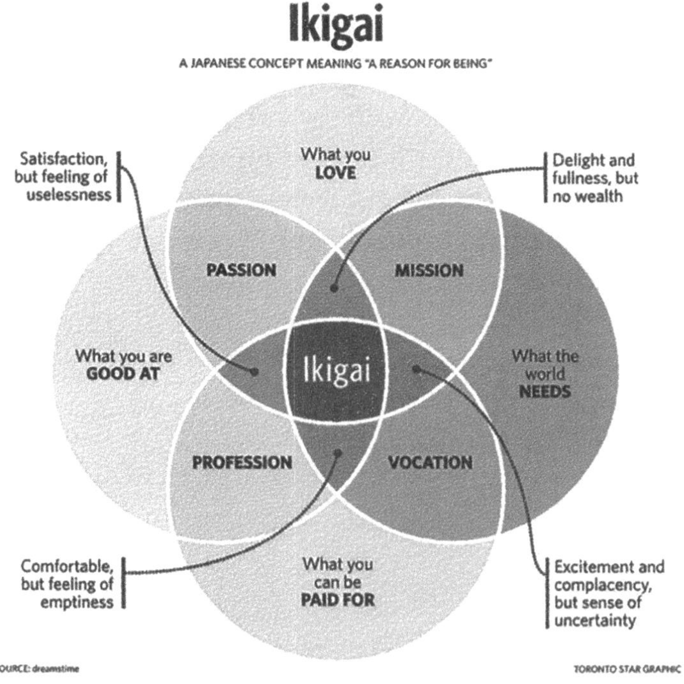

If I applied the four questions to Dr. Monica, to Oprah Monica, and CNN Monica, I would probably fall short in one or more areas. I would not find my Ikigai.

Now, let's look at corporate Monica in her leadership role. Check mark on the world needs it and paid for it. I do love what I do today. The aspect of strategizing, creating, growing a business, and developing people is fulfilling. Developing programs to help people realize their purpose professionally and personally. It's all good. And I think I'm good at it. I also have the opportunity to build programs and initiatives to support women in our company and community. And finally, this year, I started an organization to support women's education for lower-income families called the Victoria Heartstrong Organization.

Ikigai.

So, now, back to my nephew Nico. It's been a few months or so since our talk. He's started a new job in financial services where he also writes finance-related articles for The Manila Times. It's totally different from what he graduated with - Sports Science - where he thought he'd be working with professional athletes. I'm not worried though. It's still early in his own career story. We go through different paths and our own journey to find our purpose. Finding meaning and purpose in our lives is never a straight line. He will find his Ikigai.

Monica V. Maralit

Photos by Excel Panlaque for Lifestyle Asia (AGC PHC)

Monica is an advocate for women's empowerment and young women's education. At an early age, in Gainesville, Florida, she already had a calling to lead other young girls to march around the playground chanting, "Girls are better than boys!" and in high school denounce Freud's theory of "penis envy" in debate class. Monica felt that she could make a difference in people's lives by way of broadcast journalism and graduated from Ateneo de Manila University with a bachelor's degree in Communication Arts in 1997.

Monica has held leadership and management positions throughout most of her professional career. Her first leadership role started at eTelecare Global Solutions at the dawn of the Business Process Outsourcing industry in Manila, Philippines, in 2000. In Client Management, she managed multinational Fortune 500 accounts, such as American Express, Ameriprise Financial, and Sprint, in financial services and telecommunications. She now heads PSG Global Solutions and Find Human Resources in the Philippines. She has been building teams and innovating processes for recruiting for almost 15 years and helped grow PSG from 20 employees to over 4,000. If asked about a time she felt most successful in her career, she will point to the first year of the Covid-19 pandemic when she feels the true colors of the PSG culture were tested and passed with flying colors. Through the most challenging time of any company and community, the PSG family helped each other and clients without urging and provocation and with pure proactive intent to thrive.

In her roles and beyond, she has had the opportunity to build community programs such as WomenEmpowered@PSG and Project Hired. Monica has also served on the American Staffing Association's Women in Leadership Council to support multiple women-centered initiatives for the staffing industry and on the Women's Business Council of the Philippines to advocate for women's issues in business and government. She shares her experience and insights on the industry, leadership, and women's advocacies through speaking engagements.

During her free time, she loves spending time with her nieces and nephews, traveling to different destinations, practicing Vinyasa flow yoga, and teaching Sunday School. Monica credits her passion for young girls' and women's education and empowerment, volunteerism, and her fierce independence to her mother and grandmother. This year, she will open a non-profit organization called the Victoria Heartstrong Organization in their honor.

The organization aims to support underprivileged young women's education as she believes that educating women will allow them more choices in life and will help drive nation-building.

linkedin.com/in/monicamaralit
www.victoriaheartstrong.com

Shawntel Nieto

Finding One's Medicine

What medicine do you bring into this world? What are you being called to do in the midst of all of *this*?

When I was growing up, I hated being asked what I wanted to be when I grew up. I just never had an answer.

I could want to be a president, a teacher, a superstar like *Hannah Montana*, or much like what many expected me to be — a doctor like my parents, Dr. Joseph Kenneth Nieto and Dr. Virginia Girlie Nieto.

Yet, despite both the possibilities and the expectations that lay before me, I just did not know what I wanted to be.

I only truly began to figure it out by trying different things over time. I never had a predetermined "path." Instead, my path illuminated as I stepped on it. The answers I sought came as I made one decision, one choice after another.

Choices, anyway, are the alphabet — the ABCs of life. They are the means by which we paint the picture of our life, stroke by stroke, and also the means by which we derive what life and living, ultimately, means for us.

If I were to recount three choices that spelled out my life, at least as it is thus far, my ABCs would be how:

- 14 years ago, I chose to become an **A**thlete;
- 7 years ago, I chose to co-found **B**MB; and
- 3 years ago, I chose to act in the midst of the **C**ovid-19 pandemic.

These three choices, set against three important shifts in my life, led me to where and who I am today. These choices taught me to dream, to dream with a purpose, and to cultivate the courage to realize these dreams and become, to the best of my ability, a genuine woman for and with others.

A. Becoming an Athlete: Learning to Dream

When many think of me, they think of a girl who always had straight-A's. What most do not know is that after the third grade, I fell out of the honor roll because I would choose not to study for a quiz, not to participate in class, and not to pass the required reply slips I needed to for the quarter. I was very unmotivated. I did not know what I was reaching for anyway. *Why work so hard?*

It went on for some time. I never really failed, but I never excelled either.

In 2008, my mom wanted to lose weight through badminton. I joined in and played a couple of games with her. Upon seeing me on the court, my dad asked if I wanted to enroll in badminton classes that summer. I said yes.

Initially, it was only so I would "not look like a gelatin inside the court." However, I knew that, much like my brothers who were already winning championships in basketball at the time, it could be something more.

The moment I entered the badminton court, held my very first racket, and hit my first shuttlecock, I started to dream: I wanted to become a champion badminton athlete in the Philippines.

Over that summer, I trained hard; sometimes, three times a day. I did so because I wanted to be better. I started to see the value in hard work because, for the first time in my life, I understood and I resonated with the meaning behind it. All the work I was doing – all the work I was being made to do – was *for something,* and it was for **my dream.**

Fortunately, just as how one thing often leads to another, this new found ability to dream led me to dream even outside the court.

I started studying, reciting in class, and being the leader in group projects. From then on, my grades sky rocketed and I became a consistent honor student – the type my classmates would look at when the teacher was about to announce who the top scorer in an exam was.

If one asks me, "What changed?" Nothing much really. I did not get smarter. The only thing different was my ability to develop a vision of myself being someone more than I was, and how that served as fuel for me to put in the work I needed to be that.

Becoming an athlete and wanting to be the best athlete I could be taught me how to dream; and that made all the difference.

B. Starting BMB: Dreaming for Others

By 2015, I was well set as a student-athlete. I was taking up BS Management of Applied Chemistry at the Ateneo de Manila University and was the co-captain of the badminton varsity team. However, by my junior year, my friends and I randomly decided to join the Hult Prize, a student social entrepreneurship competition that came to Ateneo that year. Despite having no background whatsoever on social entrepreneurship nor business competitions, we decided to give it a shot.

Everything was going well until a week prior to the pitch day; our idea for a social enterprise was turned down. As we struggled to come up with a new idea, we were asked one simple question: **lumabas ba kayo at tinanong ang mga taong sinabi niyong tutulungan ninyo kung ano ba ang kailangan nila? (Did you go out and ask the people you said you were going to help about what they really needed?)** Our answer was: **no.** So, we were sent out to meet the very people we were trying to aid through our proposed enterprise.

We did.

We spent afternoons with impoverished communities alongside the floodway in my province of Rizal. It was there where I saw how crippling poverty was. Seeing people lack access to basic services such as electricity, water, and food shocked, saddened, and angered me at the same time. Having come to know, befriend, and truly care for the people in the communities left a desire in my core to change things.

Ever since I learned how to, dreaming has been very important to me; the ability to reach for these dreams, even more so. Yet, here were people just like myself who were probably kinder, more responsible, more mature, and more hardworking than I was who felt as if even dreaming was a luxury. The worst part is I knew why, and it all boiled down to the lottery of birth. I knew the only reason I was where I was and they were where they were was because we were born in a particular way and under particular circumstances. To me, **this can never be right.**

It is not right that anyone is deprived of access to their basic needs, to decent opportunities, or to the ability to create the life they want simply because of where and how they were born. No one deserves to be subjected to the living conditions and limitations poverty set before them.

> **It is not right that anyone is deprived of access to their basic needs, to decent opportunities, or to the ability to create the life they want simply because of where and how they were born. No one deserves to be subjected to the living conditions and limitations poverty set before them.**

Thus, the night before the competition, in prayer, I made a promise to myself: I am not leaving the communities; not until the people there *can* too.

From that point on, I started to dream not only for myself, but for others, especially those often left behind and forgotten. This was the moment I first started to fight for the alleviation of poverty in the Philippines — the moment I started ***dreaming with a purpose.***

After the Hult Prize, in order to support our partner communities gain better access to utilities such as electricity and water, my friends and I co-founded BMB Solutions. Using our knowledge on chemistry and business, we started to design and manufacture electricity-generating water filtration bikes the communities could use to gain free electricity and potable water *all through pedaling the stationary BMB bike!*

We managed to create seven working prototypes we deployed across three pilot communities.

C. Covid-19: Being and Standing as a Woman for and with Others

However, in 2018, just right when we had the business opportunity to mass produce and deploy 1000 BMB bikes to communities nationwide, my co-founders and I decided to surrender leadership over BMB. It is anticlimactic, but at that point, we were 20-year-olds who had just left university. Although we were preparing the operating line to manufacture 1000 bikes, when we truly sat down and evaluated what this could all mean for the communities, we knew the responsibility at our hands was not something we were ready for. We were deploying bikes that generated electricity and potable water. If any one of those bikes broke down or was used beyond the useable life of any of the water filters inside, someone could get hurt.

At the time, we did not have the experience nor the tools necessary to monitor and maintain what we would be deploying. Thus, as much as it pained us, especially me, to do so, we had to put the safety of the people before our own egos. Sometimes, dreaming for others does not mean bringing something to life. Sometimes, it just means choosing the best decision for everyone's sake — even if it means "failing" at what we initially set out to do.

Still, I knew I wanted to do something. I knew I wanted to help people, and although I did not become a doctor in the way my parents were, like them, I, too, wanted to provide some form of medicine in the world and serve the underserved.

In 2020, the opportunity for me to step up and address pressing social needs came about.

At the time, the Covid-19 pandemic hit and left millions of Filipinos unemployed and unable to find means to put food on the table. As a response to this, my family and I immediately started the One Cainta Food Program with the goal of providing food to 1000 people in our town, Cainta, every day. In partnership with the local government of Cainta, we were able to bring food packs to people door-to-door.

Towards the end of 2020, in partnership with community leaders, hospitals, and churches outside Cainta, we were also able to reach communities in Morong, Bulacan, and Caloocan. Slowly, we likewise got to know and build our own network of community leaders we could trust to distribute the donated goods to their communities and neighbours. This network not only allowed us to have a "neighbour to neighbour" type of participatory distribution system, but it also gave us an on-ground capacity of over 50,000 distributed packs in a day.

Looking into how we could sustain our operations despite the existence of donor fatigue, by 2021, I used our on-ground distribution brevity to introduce a new partnership scheme with organizations: *Give us your near-expiry produce, and we assure you these would be consumed days before they expire.* This proposition allowed us to be of benefit to our partner restaurants and companies, allowing them to reduce on disposal costs, while also ensuring a steady supply of food to our communities.

Up to this day – April 2023 as of writing – we are still operating daily. Thus far, we have partnered with over 80 organizations from multinationals to restaurants that provide us with donatable or overstock items, built a network of 100 community leaders that distribute our goods door-to-door, and have given 5.5 million food hampers to 700,000 people across 20 cities and 11 hospitals.

It is an admirable feat, but our program does not end there. Starting in 2021, I wanted to see how else we could support our communities. Through food, we help them get by. Yet, I also wanted to see how we could support them rise above poverty. In Filipino this translates to: "***Mula sa pagtulong sa kanilang makaraos sa pang-araw-araw, gusto rin namin silang makitang makaahon.***" Thus, to improve people's earning potential, I started our education and employment programs. By establishing partnerships with nine private schools and international fellowships, we have run weekend elective classes, tutorial services, and workshops for 2,000 public school students, as well as worked with foundations and businesses to connect 200 Persons-With-Disabilities and > 1000 mothers to livelihood capital and employment.

Beyond these social welfare programs, as deeper poverty traps remain embedded across Philippine society, I knew my work must likewise call for systemic change. **Providing social welfare on the ground is not enough; the very systems influencing the opportunities, rights, and capabilities people are given must be refined and made more equitable and livable**. As sustainability covers three pillars for development – economic, social, and environmental – I decided to use it as a framework in improving our systems in the Philippines.

For me, sustainable development is the answer if we are to advance as a country in a way that lifts everyone out of poverty *and keeps them out of it long term.*

To actionize this goal, after completing a Masters in Sustainability Management in 2019, I co-founded SustainablePH, the Society of Sustainability Practitioners (SSP), and SustainaRumble in 2020. SustainablePH builds the capacities of sustainability practitioners so they can make their cities and/or companies sustainable. Thus far, we have created Learn2Lead Sustainability, a ten-week program on sustainability management that enables professionals across sectors and industries to become sustainability managers and leaders in their work and fields.

Alongside the Society of Sustainability Practitioners, our sister non-profit that carries a membership base of over 600+ Filipino sustainability professionals, we likewise conduct a pool of sustainability experts that create and facilitate bespoke sustainability training workshops and programs for client companies and organizations who seek to start, deepen, or improve their sustainability strategies and journeys.

In order to ensure learning amongst sustainability leaders is continuous, at the Society of Sustainability Practitioners, we then host internal sustainability trainings and community engagement projects our own SSP members can attend and take part in. To cap the year off, we bring the Philippine sustainability community together through our annual Sustainability Unplugged Leadership Awards and Summit. All of this we do in order to create more sustainability leaders in the country doing good and spearheading positive change wherever it is they may be.

Meanwhile, SustainaRumble started as a podcast on sustainable development in the Philippines. Today, it is transitioning into a think-tank on sustainable development. Over the years, we have co-hosted climate hackathons, supported the government's Green Energy Option Program, and have become a permanent member of the National Economic Development Authority's Stakeholder's Chamber, advising it on national SDG-related strategies.

For my day job *(I know,"Do you still sleep?")*, I work as a sustainability consultant at Deloitte. In it, I advise both public and private organizations regarding their sustainability strategies, with a heavy focus on how organizations and businesses can mitigate social inequity and advance sustainable development in the Philippines and across the world. Currently, I work on initiatives such as the operationalization of the Circular Economy in cities and the institutionalization of equitable business initiatives amongst Philippine companies.

As I write this, I am readying myself to enter a new level in my life: that of being a student at the University of Oxford. Throughout the year I will be there, I hope to better understand how else we could design policies, programs, and systems in order to make these more equitable. In short, I want to know — beyond all I do now, what else is out there that we might be able to bring in and adopt here so we can further make life easier, better, and more equitable for Filipinos?

Seven years ago, I made a promise not to leave the communities until the people there could, too. Today, my dream — my promise is different: **it is to help create a community no one needs to leave anymore.**

It is a lot of work, and my days often end at 3:00 a.m. To me, however, it is all worth it. It is worth it not just because this is my dream but because I believe in the purpose and the mission driving this dream. At the end of the day, ***this*** is who I am now. To the best of my ability, I try to live and offer my life as one of a woman for and with others — one who continues to believe that everyone has the right to a decent life, that poverty in the Philippines is not inevitable, and that we all carry within ourselves the ability and the responsibility to care for each other and for the world.

Stringing It Together: *My medicine*

So how did I discover what medicine it is that I brought to the world?

It is by simply going through life actively searching not for the exact medicine I can offer, but, instead, of ways and opportunities through which I could be of service to others and to what is greater than me. Everything else, the solutions, initiatives, or *medicine,* follows.

As evident in my story, I never planned for any of these things to happen. I never planned on becoming an athlete, a social entrepreneur, or a sustainability leader. I never planned on committing to work to eradicate poverty in the Philippines through advancing sustainable development nationwide.

However, as time went on and I pursued the different opportunities that presented themselves to me, I understood *to my core* that this was the path that resonated most with me; and thus, although it may not be the easiest, most conventional, nor safest path to trek, it is one I wholeheartedly continue to work on.

The path illuminated and continues to illuminate only as I step on it; and the *purpose* I constantly seek only really becomes clearer with every decision I make. At times, I get it right; other times, I get it wrong. Yet, in the end, I have come to understand that so long as I keep my my values clear, my mind open to feedback and introspection, and my discipline intact, the dots always do connect. In the end, each decision and circumstance will lead me more and more towards who I truly am and how best I could contribute in this world.

"The path illuminated and continues to illuminate only as I step on it; and the purpose I constantly seek only really becomes clearer with every decision I make. At times, I get it right; other times, I get it wrong. Yet, in the end, I have come to understand that so long as I keep my my values clear, my mind open to feedback and introspection, and my discipline intact, the dots always do connect. In the end, each decision and circumstance will lead me more and more towards who I truly am and how best I could contribute in this world.

It truly only is in going out there and trying to contribute in whatever way we can and are being given the opportunity to that we begin to understand ourselves and the medicines we can offer to the world more.

These medicines do not have to be grand and will always look different for each and every person. However, I hope it brings everyone, especially those currently *soul searching*, comfort knowing that it is always there. We always have the capacity to do and contribute something good to the world. We only have to look inside of us and then dare to venture beyond ourselves to find, cultivate, and provide it.

These medicines may change and multiply over time, as it has for me then and as will be the case if and when, for instance, I become a wife and a mother; but the desire to cultivate and offer it must not.

That is the true call. It is not to identify any one single purpose or medicine in life. Instead, it is to constantly carry with us the ***sense of having a purpose*** — of offering a medicine wherever it is we are, and then ***tapping and re-tapping into this sense of purpose*** as we go along and face the various circumstances and opportunities we will in life.

This is how I began to cultivate the medicines I currently offer to the world. I simply answered the different calls to service I could hear at the time. This is what I implore everyone else to do as well.

Once more, we all *always* have the capacity and the responsibility to care for the world. We must simply make the choice to act and do so now.

Shawntel Nieto

Shawntel is the co-Founder and President of Sustainable PH Inc., and of the One Cainta Food Program. She is likewise a co-founder SustainaRumble! and the Society of Sustainability Practitioners, a TV host under IBC Channel 13, and a consultant under Deloitte's Climate and Sustainability team. She is currently taking up her Masters in Public Policy at the University of Oxford, with the support of the Oxford Weidenfeld Hoffmann scholarship. Shawntel is the very first Filipino to receive this prestigious scholarship.

Through the organizations she has co-founded, she has provided food, water, disaster relief, sup- plementary education, and livelihood opportunities to over 700,000 people across 20 cities and 11 hospitals in the Philippines. She obtained her Bachelors in Management of Applied Chemistry as the *program awardee* (degree valedictorian) in 2017 and her Masters in Sustainability Management in 2019. She has worked as a researcher focused on social entrepreneurship and sustainability, as a corporate analyst under JP Morgan & Chase Inc., and as the Philippine country manager of CSRWorks International, a Singapore-based sustainability consulting firm.

For her work over the past seven years, she has been selected as a Dalai Lama Fellow and One Young World Scholar, was awarded the (Princess) Diana Award, was selected as one of the Philippines' Ten Outstanding Young Men and Women (TOYM) for 2022, and was listed as a Forbes 30 Under 30 Honoree for Social Impact.

Arizza Nocum

Never Enough No More: A Little Girl Dreams of Peace

"You can do anything you want in your life, as long as you're the best at it. You can be a lawyer, teacher, banker, nurse, but you have to be at the top of your field. You can even wash laundry – just make sure you're #1 in the world at washing laundry!"

I remember my dad telling me this during a mealtime conversation as a little girl. Though that conversation happened 15 or 20 years ago, I've not forgotten it. It's probably because I hated doing chores at home and could not fathom ever dedicating my life to washing laundry. Or perhaps it was because that was the moment that best represented the kind of philosophy my parents instilled in me as I was growing up.

This philosophy of being the best has pushed and fueled me to accomplish things I never thought I could accomplish, but it has also pulled me down in ways that would become more visible as the years went on.

If I wasn't the best, it was never enough.

Racing to the Top

Since my first year in school, I've been honed to compete for #1. I was encouraged to read as many books as I could so I could learn faster than all my other classmates. I usually ranked first in my section in terms of grades. I joined – and won – numerous competitions in school, everything from *Munting Mutya* ("Little Muse") to inter-school math contests to Boggle tournaments to quiz bees. I was student council president and valedictorian in sixth grade.

High school was a slightly different story. I got a full scholarship to study at arguably the top high school in the Philippines, and my schoolmates and I were seen as the "cream of the crop." My fellow classmates were real geniuses: kids who'd had asteroids named after them after winning international physics competitions, classmates who had published books at age 12, kids who were in national varsity leagues, and math savants who were already doing college calculus.

In primary school, I could probably have been seen as the best. But in high school, I was *normal.* That pushed me even harder to reach the standard my parents expected of me.

I wasn't the best at math or sciences – subjects my high school focused on – but I had my fair share of wins. I topped a national standard test on social studies. I had essays published in newspapers. I became vice president of the student council. I was selected to go to India for an international leadership conference. I received the leadership medal during graduation.

Thanks to the privilege of my past academic life, I finished Top 50 nationwide in the University of the Philippines College Admissions Test (UPCAT) and received the Oblation Scholarship, which meant a full scholarship, monthly stipend, book allowances, and even occasional dinners with the school chancellor.

I took up Industrial Engineering and felt a need to prove myself as a young woman in a sea of men in the halls of engineering college, and so I did. I graduated magna cum laude (with high honors); I represented my school and country in competitions and events in the U.S., Indonesia, and Thailand; and I was one of three recipients of the Chancellor's Merit Award selected from thousands of graduating students.

Despite all these, I remember feeling sad during my college graduation because I didn't graduate summa cum laude (with highest honors), and I had to look on as each of those seemingly godlike students received their diplomas on stage.

Competing at school wasn't enough though, and I knew – and my parents knew – that I had more to offer beyond the confines of my classroom.

Widening my Reach

If you're wondering about the rest of my family, we were all part of the same program. My dad was a multi-award-winning journalist and later became a coveted media consultant. My mom started and managed multiple businesses. My younger sister was a junior golf athlete, competed internationally from age 5, finished fifth in a world tournament, and has six holes-in-one.

But there was something about my family that was more peculiar than our collective exhaustion towards excellence. This strange element had provided the seed that helped me grow beyond school into a role that pushed me further on a path to "greatness," and that has unexpectedly defined nearly 15 years of my life.

This peculiar trait about my family is that it has two religions.

My mom is a Muslim woman from the Tausug tribe of Sulu, and my dad is a former seminarian from a conservative Roman Catholic family in Zamboanga. Their marriage looked out of place against the backdrop of conflict, terrorism, and war in Southern Philippines (which includes their hometowns).

Their stubborn determination to be the best was not confined to their careers. Despite the fears of their relatives and the judgment of people around them, they stayed together, started a family, and decided to build a home with two faiths.

To this day, our family learns from both the Bible and the Quran, celebrates both Christmas and Ramadan, and spends time with Catholic relatives on my dad's side and Muslim relatives on my mom's side.

I learned a lot growing up like this. I learned how important things like respect and empathy are. I learned how little things can mean so much, such as how not having any religious objects at home made it feel like a neutral and safe place for all of us. Most of all, I learned that despite all the conflict that was happening in the Philippines and in the world at that time, peace is still possible.

KRIS was born from that idea.

In 2008, I was in high school when I co-founded Kristiyano Islam Peace Library or KRIS, a non-profit organization promoting peace through education and youth leadership. As a young leader and as someone who's benefited from the privilege of an education, I knew how important both of these dimensions were to my growth as a person. And I believed, deep down, that being the best version of myself would make the world a better and more peaceful place. That's what I wanted for other young Filipinos, especially those who had grown up in communities affected by conflict and poverty.

In the first years of our journey at KRIS, we were able to build 6 libraries, provide 400 scholarship grants to students from preschool to university, and donate thousands of books and computers to communities affected by conflict and poverty.

It's been a whirlwind of a journey since we started nearly 15 years ago, but I'm proud to say that today, KRIS continues its mission. From 2020 – 2022, we trained more than 1,000 young leaders on peacebuilding, provided seed grants from PHP 30,000 – 50,000 ($600 – $1,000) to youth organizations around the Philippines that had promising ideas for peace that they wanted to execute, and reached hundreds of thousands through our online and offline information campaigns. During the pandemic, we were also able to provide tablets and educational materials to 70 students in need for online learning, and we leveraged our network of young people to provide food, medicines, clothing, and more to 3,280 individuals affected by typhoons and flooding in the Philippines in late 2022.

Hurting from the Fall

If I'm being honest, this "best version of myself" that I wanted to model to all the amazing young people I've worked with through the years at KRIS was not really my best – especially at the beginning.

When I started working on KRIS slavishly in high school and then in college, I reveled at the accomplishment of being thrust into the limelight because of my advocacy. I received multiple awards here and abroad, was invited to speak in front of hundreds or thousands in conferences all over the world, was featured in multiple publications, and delighted at the notion of being able to work with prestigious organizations and personalities that I'd only read about in books. I felt utter joy even from just typing in another line in my resume. On social media, I would go viral with write-ups about my work with one article even getting translated into multiple languages.

One side of me felt that I had *made* it, that I was *the best*, finally.

But one side of me felt that it was *never enough*. I needed to work harder. I needed to hit more targets. I needed to be excellent both at school and at KRIS. I needed to be a model student. I needed to get more volunteers. I needed to be a better public speaker. I needed to push our story to more publications. I needed more followers online. I needed to add more lines to my resume. I needed to figure out more ways to raise funds. Heck, I needed to win the Nobel Prize for Peace because, if I could go for it, why not?

So I pushed myself to the bone. I would barely sleep. I'd work until I felt sick. I didn't value my relationships with people. I'd measure myself against everyone. I forced myself to go on and on and on until, after graduating from college, I slowly dug myself into a hole of burnout and frustration and pressure and anxiety and sadness that I almost didn't get out of.

At my lowest point, I thought: *I will never be enough.*

But the path I took through KRIS that led to this point also somehow saved me in the end.

Working with KRIS may have catapulted me into a stage where I could truly be *the best*, but it has simultaneously emptied "*the best*" of its meaning. And that … that is the actual best thing that has ever happened to me.

Working with KRIS may have catapulted me into a stage where I could truly be the best, but it has simultaneously emptied "the best" of its meaning. And that … that is the actual best thing that has ever happened to me.

All the awards meant nothing beside the fact that I could actually help another young person go to school and live a fuller life. Getting my name in a newspaper felt worthless when there were so many bright children out there who still couldn't read. My resume is just a scrap of paper when I think about all the privileges I've had versus all the challenges faced by the students we worked with in war-torn places like Zamboanga, Sulu, Basilan, and Marawi.

Truly believing, deep down, that the best versions of other kids like me would make the world a better place pushed me to see the intelligence, courage, creativity, and hope that all these youth innately have. I realized I wasn't working to make them the best versions of themselves. I was just working to unleash the things they already had in them.

And if I could believe that all young women and men inherently carried greatness already, then I could also believe in my own greatness.

I may not win the Nobel Prize or write the next great book of the Philippines or start the world's #1 non-profit, but I have to grow to be proud, content, and happy with what I've accomplished and with where I am in life.

Now I say to myself: I am never *enough*, because I am *more than enough.*

Journeying towards Peace

My longest job so far has been to work for peace in areas affected by conflict, but I never thought that one peace that I truly lacked was an inner peace. Slowly, painfully, I've learned to teach myself that I, as a woman, am enough. I can keep dreaming and working – and I still have so many targets and deadlines and dreams ahead – but, for now, I am enough.

Women and girls elsewhere need to teach themselves that they are more than enough, despite the demands heaped on them by their families, friends, social media, society, and even themselves.

Being enough means being kind to myself, taking a break when I need to, saying nice things to myself, getting enough sleep, enjoying my relationships with family and loved ones, and living *my* dream even if it may not be the *best* dream out there.

Don't get me wrong. This journey towards being the best has taught me so much, and I will forever be grateful to my parents for pushing me on a path that has been anything but easy.

But if I could go pick up from that conversation with my dad about being the #1 laundromat some 15 or 20 years ago, I would tell him this:

As an adult, I've learned many things. One very important lesson is that washing laundry is an extremely difficult task, so if you're #1 at washing laundry in the world, then it's an astronomical achievement.

You're right. You can do anything you want in your life, but only as long as you know you're more than enough. You can be a lawyer, teacher, banker, nurse, and you can be at the top of your field – or you can be happy

> **“You're right. You can do anything you want in your life, but only as long as you know you're more than enough. You can be a lawyer, teacher, banker, nurse, and you can be at the top of your field – or you can be happy where you are. On the way to the top, at the sidelines, out of the game. It's up to you.**

where you are. On the way to the top, at the sidelines, out of the game. It's up to you. You can even wash laundry. You don't necessarily have to be #1 at washing laundry in the world, but you certainly have to be #1 in believing, trusting, and loving yourself wherever you find yourself in life.

Arizza Nocum

Arizza is the co-founder and president of KRIS, a non-profit organization that promotes peace through education and youth leadership. KRIS has trained over 1,000 Filipino youth leaders on peacebuilding, supported hundreds of youth and youth organizations in their initiatives for education and development, and reached millions through its education campaigns. In 2021, KRIS was recognized as one of Ten Accomplished Youth Organizations (TAYO) in the Philippines.

Arizza is also one of ten young leaders hand-picked by the former United Nations Secretary-General Kofi Annan to eradicate violent extremism through the global Extremely Together initiative. For her work, Arizza was recognized as one of the Ten Outstanding Students of the Philippines in 2016 and one of five global recipients of Zonta International's Young Women for Public Affairs Award.

She is also the Managing Director of DIGInspire, a communications agency providing strategic marketing services to top companies across diverse industries in the Philippines.

Web: arizzanocum.com
LinkedIn: linkedin.com/in/arizza-nocum-b5a47444

Paulynn Paredes Sicam

MY VARIEGATED LIFE

I have been a teacher, a reporter, an opinion columnist, a human rights educator, a peace negotiator, and a book editor. In school, I acted on stage, wrote for the school paper, and represented my college in inter-school student events. I am also an activist who joined protests during the martial law period, and came forward for human rights, press freedom, women's rights, and good governance, among other urgent causes. Finally, I am a wife, mother to two daughters, and grandmother to two grown boys and a teenage girl.

But probably the most important part of me is where I came from. I am my father and mother's third daughter, the sixth of their ten children – the classic middle child in a rambunctious family who had to strive to be seen and heard in the competitive environment at home.

My father was an intellectual, a lawyer who represented Catholic schools in their dealings with the Philippine government; a law professor who taught nights in two schools, delivered nightly commentaries on radio on socio-political matters, and wrote speeches for President Ramon Magsaysay as his ghost writer.

As a dedicated public servant, my father didn't earn much, so my mother handled the household frugally. She sewed our clothes, knitted our socks and sweaters, cut our hair, baked cakes and cookies, changed lightbulbs, and drove a d tinkered with the family car. She also supervised the building of our home.

I was ten years old in 1957 when my dad perished in the airplane crash on a mountainside in Cebu province that killed President Magsaysay and 21 others. With ten children to clothe, feed, and send to school, Mom had too much on her plate, but she soldiered on and learned the ropes of the insurance business. We survived.

Mom was strong-willed, a fighter. She could do anything she put her mind to. She would surprise us decades later when we got an urgent call early one morning that she had been arrested by the martial law police. But that is getting ahead of my story.

I did well in school where I majored in English Literature and wrote for the school paper. But upon graduating, I had no idea what I wanted to do, so I opted to postpone my future by signing up to teach in the wilds of Mindanao. I was accepted as an English teacher in a parochial school in Barrio Diatagon, Lianga, Surigao del Sur.

I taught for one school year in a two-story wooden structure built on a field that was water-logged most of the time.

I handled subjects that were required by the Department of Education such as English Composition and English Literature across the board for all high school students in the country, even those in the barrios who were barely acquainted with the English language. But I managed. When I had to introduce them to Homer's Iliad and Odyssey, and even the most elementary of poems in English, I didn't bother to require them to read. Instead, I acted out the stories, taking on the roles of the characters. I got my most delinquent student to memorize the poem Invictus, and recite it at a school program, for which he got a standing ovation. They learned English words that I helped them interpret in their language.

When I returned to Manila after a year in the barrio, I was far from the sheltered college girl who had left school just a year before. I had seen life in the backwater, the swamps and forests of Surigao. Now, back in the city, I had a hard time fitting in. I applied to advertising agencies as a copy writer. But the people who interviewed me were too smart and glib, their glass and chrome offices too sleek. Fresh from the barrio, I didn't want to go there. I didn't want to go back to teaching either. My year in Diatagon had left me traumatized.

I heard that the Manila Chronicle Magazine was in need of an editorial assistant, so I presented myself as an English major from a convent school with no portfolio but a story to tell about how I spent my first year out of college. The editor, a crusty old timer who growled when he spoke, told me to write about my year teaching in Surigao del Sur. I got the job as a "go-fer" in the weekly magazine.

The Chronicle office in an old pre-war building in Intramuros was grubby. Desks were piled with old newsprint, books, and magazines along with unwashed cups of coffee and ashtrays filled with cigarette butts. The air reeked of cigarette smoke, and my co-workers threw friendly curses across the room. But they were real people, and they were welcoming, and I felt right at home.

It was heady. Ater a couple of months doing grunge work putting out the magazine, I was discovered by the news desk which put me in the thick of things as a feature writer and reporter covering personalities, including Imelda Marcos, meeting politicians, attending fashion shows and cocktail parties, and reviewing stage plays, when I wasn't out in the streets following student demonstrators and dodging the violence that almost always occurred between the students and the police.

Journalism kept me fully occupied. I loved my job and struggled to balance my time between journalism and motherhood. I had gotten married in 1970 and had my first child a year later. It must have been because I was now a mother that I was "promoted" to a desk job as a section editor.

My daughter Monica was one year old when martial law was declared in the country on September 21, 1972. All media offices, including the Chronicle, were shut down. Radio and TV stations were silenced, replaced by new stations and publications owned and run by persons related or close to the dictator's family.

My husband and I, both in the media, lost our jobs. Survival was the name of the game, but joining the new publications that operated under censorship by the new dispensation was out of the question. However, I accepted a job in government as a writer of memos and speeches for the Secretary of Agriculture who was a family friend.

In 1975, I was asked to conceptualize and co-edit a quarterly general interest magazine called Goodman. It was a glossy PR publication for a car company. It was the height of martial law, and the controlled media had become listless, tired, and boring. Goodman made a difference. Designed by Nik Ricio, a graphic artist who went on to design award-winning coffee table books, we ran feature stories, personality profiles, even literary pieces and photo essays that caught the public's interest and garnered awards. The magazine ran for a good two years until the car company ran out of PR funds.

Although I had been a conscientious but discreet objector to martial law, my life took a strange turn in 1980 when our mother joined a group of urban guerrillas who disrupted the martial law regime by burning business establishments belonging to cronies of the dictator. They were found out, arrested, detained, and sentenced to death by a military court. I finally dove openly into the protest movement, campaigning for human rights, organizing rallies, producing placards and leaflets, and appealing to government officials demanding the release of political prisoners.

Mercifully, the death sentence on Mom's group had not yet been executed in 1986 when the People Power Revolution sent the dictator into exile and democracy was restored by President Cory Aquino. My mother was released along with other political detainees, and their cases were thrown out. Some 20 years later, Mom was proclaimed a martial law hero, her name inscribed on the granite Wall of Heroes at the Bantayog ng mga Bayani in Quezon City.

The 14 years of martial law tested my survival instinct. I kept reminding myself that I was my mother's daughter and could handle whatever fate threw at me. I was a freelance writer who accepted almost every job that came my way to help pay the rent. Among my assignments, I had to interview the Dictator's daughter, Imee Marcos, two different times. In 1981, Imee asked me to interview her father, President Marcos himself. She wanted me to elicit something fresh and human from him, nothing political or controversial, just a

"The 14 years of martial law tested my survival instinct. I kept reminding myself that I was my mother's daughter and could handle whatever fate threw at me.

relaxed conversation about his youth, his hobbies, his dreams, and his family. I protested that my mother was detained as a political prisoner charged with allegedly plotting to kill her father (she didn't), but it was martial law and Imee got her way. I had no choice but to interview the dictator.

It was in the presidential office, sitting behind a desk that towered over the rest of the room, where President Marcos, describing his children one by one, confided that Imee was his "intellectual twin," Irene was "everybody's sweetheart," and Bongbong, well, he paused and said, "He has good muscle coordination." Then, he added that "like his mother," Bongbong liked to party. Bongbong is Ferdinand Marcos Jr., who is now president of the Philippines.

Marcos also reminisced about his infamous war record which I did not dare question. But when I was given a video tape of the interview by the Malacañang press office, I asked a family friend who was close to the president, to tell me how much of his war stories were true. The verdict? Forty percent.

How does one write about such a conversation without a wink and a smirk that would alert the censors? I decided to publish the entire interview verbatim, in Q and A format, without comment.

Journalism was a tightrope. Editors were careful not to publish stories that were even slightly critical of the first family and the regime. We watched our words, but it did not stop us from covering stories that bordered on the "subversive." I found a home and lifelong friends in a group of women writers who got together to push back against the restrictions of the martial law regime, challenging the limits of censorship by covering stories that most editors felt were best left untold. We called ourselves WOMEN, for Women Writers in Media NOW. Some of our members were actually summoned by a military commission and questioned about their choice of stories. Forty plus years later, we are still together, each member continuing to shine in her own incomparable way.

In 1984, I was awarded a journalism fellowship at Stanford University by The Asia Foundation. With my family in tow, I took a year-long sabbatical in the resort-like campus in Palo Alto, California. It was a good break from the political tensions at home. The protest movement had swelled after the murder of Ninoy Aquino in August 1983, and we were starting to smell the stench of a dying regime. In Stanford, I did my share speaking before student and civic audiences about the excesses of the Marcos dictatorship.

The Chronicle was resurrected after the EDSA Revolution in February 1986 that drove the dictator, his family and his cronies into exile. I returned to the paper as a senior reporter covering urgent issues in the democratic restoration such as the communist insurgency, human rights, agrarian reform, the peace process, and electoral participation. I was also stringing for Western publications such as the New York Times and the Christian Science Monitor. I had started writing my column, Heart and Mind, which was well received by what were then called the "middle forces" – not right-wing or left-wing, but firmly committed to the restoration of our freedoms, justice and democracy.

It was the best of times to be in the media, being part of the national effort to rebuild our damaged democracy. It was also the worst of times. Our democracy was being challenged by renegade military officers who mounted no less than seven coup attempts against the Cory Aquino government. Rebuilding and protecting democracy was not a walk in the park.

I was promoted to editor of the editorial pages, writing editorials and my column, and shepherding the Chronicle's many columnists. I also edited the paper's Sunday Special supplement that featured in-depth analyses of the events of the week. The paper had started to go digital. It was an exciting time putting out pages using the new technology.

Late in 1989, I received word that my editor wanted me to take advantage of a generous retirement package being offered by the company. I was shocked and upset. What had I done that he wanted me out? When I refused to resign, he fired me, rudely interrupting a promising career that I thought I wouldn't mind growing old in. From my high perch in the paper, I landed with a thud, bitter and broken-hearted.

And thus, the rest of my life unfurled in unexpected directions.

I received a call from President Cory Aquino offering me a position in government as a member of the five-person Commission on Human Rights. Human rights was an issue I had been reporting on with a passion, so, the President said, I should put my money where my mouth was. Of course, I said yes. It would only be for four years, and I had no other immediate option. Also, I was too invested in the restoration of democracy to refuse my President's challenge.

Human rights work was a totally different ballgame. I had much to learn about the law. I had to promote human rights as universal, indivisible, inalienable and respectful of the equality and dignity of every person. But I was speaking to an audience of soldiers and policemen who were suspicious of human rights per se. The armed services, who had to fight the Communist Party of the Philippines and the New People's Army, were particularly hostile to human rights laws which they regarded as partial to the CPP-NPA. Human rights, they believed, applied only to enemies of the state and not to soldiers and policemen whose job it is to protect the State.

They had to understand that human rights apply to everyone, be they soldiers or rebels. However, since it is the duty of government to protect the human rights of every individual, as agents of the state, soldiers and policemen who abuse their authority commit human right violations. It was a difficult concept for them to follow. I needed a less legalistic approach.

I gathered a group of educators, psychologists, lawyers, and human rights experts to fashion a program that would "humanize" our approach to human rights education to reach the hardened hearts and minds of the armed services. We veered away from formal lectures on human rights law and history that made audiences fall asleep, and spoke directly to their humanity.

It was a novel approach that had positive results. Officers who were once closed-minded were open to discussion, some shedding their long-held beliefs, even actually admitting their errors in the past. But it involved a lot of work and was difficult to sustain. After I retired from the Commission, the program was discontinued. But the UNESCO gave the CHR the Human Rights Education award in 1994.

In 1996, I was invited to join an ambitious regional civil society initiative to try and open the governments in the ASEAN region, which are generally hostile to human rights, to discussions leading to the establishment of an ASEAN Human Rights Mechanism. It has been a protracted struggle but the group soldiers on, hoping for better times under ASEAN leaders who are more open to the concept and practice of human rights.

My retirement from the CHR brought me to new but related territory. The government was pursuing a peace process with the Communist Party of the Philippines, and I was invited to be an adviser to the government's peace panel on human rights matters. As a reporter, I had covered the failed peace negotiations between the government and the CPP-NPA-NDF in 1986-87 where I got to know its leading personalities. Furthermore, visiting my mother in Bicutan during her political detention, I had access to her fellow martial law detainees who were leaders of the Party. I was sufficiently informed about the Party and the communist movement to be of use to the government peace panel.

I stayed in the peace process for the next 20 years (1995 to 2015) where I also served as a member of the panel's technical committee and the government negotiating panel. I watched the prospects of a genuine peace agreement rise and fall through three presidencies

(Ramos, Arroyo and Aquino III). My realization is that the parties were never on the same plane at the same time, no meeting of minds and hearts to compromise for the sake of the Filipino people who desired an end to a violent insurgency that has now lasted over 50 years.

In 1994, after a four-year hiatus when I was at the CHR, I resumed writing my column, Heart and Mind. I hopped from newspaper to newspaper looking for a hospitable home, until finally settling in at the Philippine Star where I was placed in the only space available -- in the Lifestyle section. It was a pleasant place to be at first. My editor gave me the freedom to write what I wanted. But being a political person with irrepressible views, the gods of the paper realized that some of my views had no place in Lifestyle and had to be toned down or actually censored. I tried to conform with the editorial strictures, but at the onset of Covid 19 early in 2020, my world as I knew it stopped. Amid the haze, uncertainty and boredom of the pandemic, I gave up my column and have not resumed it since.

At 77 and in semi-retirement, I am kept busy editing book manuscripts for publication. However, I see myself as primarily a journalist. I have covered protests, massacres, even an execution. I have seen political leaders squabble over power and prestige. I have seen communities of informal settlers lose their homes in violent demolitions, and tenant farmers fighting to protect their farms from agricultural and real estate developers. I have seen hopes for change and good governance dashed by dishonest politicians manipulating the electoral system. I have also seen a people rise and prevail against an entrenched dictator.

I have been privileged to witness a lot of my nation's history from different vantage points which has given me a good appreciation of what still need to be done for my country and people. I am inspired to push on by my two daughters.

"I have been privileged to witness a lot of my nation's history from different vantage points which has given me a good appreciation of what still need to be done for my country and people.

In 1985, as we prepared to leave Stanford after my fellowship, my husband broached the idea of applying for political asylum, what with martial law still in full force in the country. My daughters protested saying, "We only signed up for a year. Besides, we have a country to liberate." They were 14 and 10 years old.

Seventeen years ago, when I turned 60, I was persuaded by a publisher to collect my best columns and compile them into a book. Although I have edited and produced many books for others, this 17-year old volume is the only one I have produced for myself. I dedicated the book to Monica and Glory, writing: "…whose welfare and future have guided all of my life choices."

I wasn't always around when they needed me, but they were always part of my work. They came to coverages, hung out in the newsroom, made placards, marched in demonstrations and rallies, met political detainees and mentored and played with their children. In the intro to my book that I asked them to write, they described me as "the farthest thing from anyone's idea of typical mother." And Glory shared that the discussions between us could swing from an analysis of the political situation to whatever shallow drama was going on in her life.

Monica wrote: "I am very much my mother's daughter in the things that I have chosen to do. I've realized that I cannot take on a job that is not associated with a cause—not with an upbringing like mine!"

In the many roles I have undertaken, the many accomplishments I have been credited with, I consider my daughters to be my best work. I take pride in the strong and principled women they have become -- like their courageous grandmother who made me who I am, and who even stood up to the dictator -- and the generations of strong atypical mothers who preceded us.

September 11, 2023

Paulynn Paredes Sicam

Paulynn Paredes Sicam was a journalist, reporter, columnist, and editor for over 50 years. She was also a member of the Philippine Commission on Human Rights, a human rights educator at the Benigno Aquino Foundation, and a consultant and later member of the Philippine Government panel for peace negotiations with the Communist Party of the Philippines. She wrote post-presidency speeches for President Corazon Aquino, as well.

In 1984, she was a John S. Knight Journalism Fellow at Stanford University. She is a member of the TOWNS Foundation, having been awarded as an Outstanding Woman in the Nation's Service for Journalism in 1989. She also received the Freedom Flame Award for her human rights work in the Southeast Asian Region from the Friedrich Naumann Foundation in 2016. In retirement, she continues to accept writing and editing assignments, including seeing books through production and publication. She is a proud mother of two daughters and grandmother to three grandchildren.

She can be reached at meiling1316@gmail.com

Unyx Sta. Ana

Stepping Forward Into Our Own Shoes

A. Coming Home

Who am I? What makes me unique? How can I make a difference? These are questions I asked myself as a kid.

I was born in a family that has been making shoes since 1887 with five generations in total. While I knew that we have been making shoes for a long time, I did not know how big of a deal it was. As a late comer kid, I only have observed how our family had lost its foothold in the industry and how the business was both a source of pride and downfall for us. As our success dwindled, it was a struggle to keep up with the business of shoes, but our love for the craft was also what we held onto.

When I was seven, my father wrote me a letter saying, "I hope that one day, you can be one of the best shoemakers in the country, and that you will bring back the honor of your ancestors." Looking back now, I did not understand its gravity, but it was a heavy responsibility to be passed on to a seven-year-old child who is also his youngest and only daughter. My father will always tell me about the good memories of our legacy tracing back to my great-great-grandfather who took part in the founding of the local shoe industry in Marikina City during the Spanish era. As a naive child thinking that with our history, doing so would not be so difficult, I told myself that one day, I can bring that honor back. Little did I know, it was a heavy burden to carry. It was not only getting into the industry, but it was also the unraveling of the complex dynamics of being part of the shoemaking family, including how it led to our financial struggles and indifferences toward each other, all coming from a painful past rooted in the patriarchal upbringing of my grandfather that we all never had the opportunity to heal from.

As I grew up, I began to understand the complications of our family relationship with shoes. I knew that I had to build my own name, away from our surname and essentially move on from the past and start anew without the burden of our lineage. Being an innate geek, I was always fascinated with how I can code to solve real world problems.

I wanted to build software for good governance and social progress. Fortunately, I successfully managed to finish my Computer Science degree as a part-time working student aided by a scholarship.

I knew that aside from building software, I also wanted to start my own business. From working for Microsoft, I eventually became a technopreneur. Together with my friend from college, I founded my first company that automated tracking of advertising in real-time, using audio matching technology. We started it from scratch to profitability until it was acquired. Throughout my founder journey, I built my own network and explored the possibilities of the space I was in. I also served as a trusted partner alongside notable industry leaders building startups and serving the largest enterprises in the country towards its digital transformation.

I was devoted to my career, to the ideas that I could build, and to the solutions I could provide. At that time, I was already far from where I started, and I was on top of my game as a technopreneur until my father who was a retired shoemaker got into an accident. The incident had me thinking, from more than a century old tradition, from a legacy that I grew up learning about, who will then follow in his footsteps? I realized that this dilemma is not unique to me but is shared by an entire industry with its craft slowly diminishing. From there on, I found myself part of the beautiful but also complex world of footwear as a founder of Zapateria.

Taking leadership and ownership as the fifth generation of our family heritage and being a woman to do so in a once-upon-a-time male dominated industry, I started Zapateria to serve as the Philippines' first creative hub for footwear design and development with a mission to foster creativity and innovation for the new and future generations to come. Reality struck hard though that honoring our heritage also came with the discovery of the untangled family traumas from a legacy that no one seemed to want anymore. As challenging as it was, over time, I realized that what I was running away from was something that I had to run back into in order to understand myself and why our family, particularly my father, was so passionate about shoes despite the pain and hardship it brought to us. By being surrounded by a community of like-minded individuals that made up my chosen family through Zapateria, my new so-called home has shaped me more holistically to see myself and the world differently with more meaning, purpose and empathy.

B. Crafting Soulfully

Building a community of individuals with shared core values and passion for our craft did not happen overnight. While it helped that our forefathers were into shoemaking, on my own founding Zapateria, I still needed to introduce new ways of thinking and collaborating into the old school industry. The hardest part was infusing the agile nature, dynamism, and diversity of the startup scene into the authenticity and humanity of our 136-year old heritage. However, I learned that before I can even affect change or impose on changing a culture of an industry that had lost its prime, I apparently needed to first immerse myself into the craft and love shoes completely, and wholeheartedly make it part of who I am in my own terms.

Loving our Own

I remember the days when my father and I used to argue a lot about tools, materials, components, and techniques used in shoemaking. Oftentimes, I would compare our handmade process to those abroad versus what we have employed for decades because of my limited exposure to our unique local artistry. It was only when I began to learn the craft myself that I developed a deeper appreciation for our own ways of making. While learning from other countries can help diversify our methods, there is also a lot to be proud of about Filipino craftsmanship, especially through the lenses of our very best artisans who put their hearts in every pair they create.

Most of our skilled makers today have gained their expertise through years of practice by learning on their own. The knowledge and wisdom they have gathered cannot simply be taught in theory. Our craft is also an exercise of resourcefulness and resilience as we had to make use of what we have due to the lack of special tools, materials, and heavy machinery locally. This empowered our capabilities in making beautiful and globally competitive footwear by hand.

From then on, I did not have to bother comparing what we do or what we have from the rest of the world. I am proud that we have our own shoemaking heritage, a craftsmanship we can call our own while keeping an open mind in redefining standards. By this time, I learned that the first step is not to try to be anybody else and just love who we are first. There is no such a thing as perfect, too. We can always strive to do better, but we can also embrace imperfections. Because of shoes and my exposure to Filipino ingenuity, it was clear that our success as a nation starts with how we can support and appreciate what we get from our own backyard.

Keeping Pace

From a technology enterprise worldview, there is this pressure of scaling fast and big as if economic success and life's worth depend on it. Agility is vital because of the ever changing landscape of technology. If you cannot keep up or be one step ahead, you will be left behind. In my younger years, this fast-paced lifestyle came easily to me. I enjoyed working from "dusk till dawn," constantly ticking off accomplishments to make room for the next ones. Always striving to go and grow bigger for my ventures. In time though, I realized that it also came with the unnecessary strain of always having to move. I barely had time to sit and reflect or process what I was putting my mind and body through.

Immersing myself into craft, I realized the importance of slow and steady. Shoes require patience and also an appreciation of proper timing. A good analogy of this is how when making shoes, you need to wait for the adhesives to dry just enough to ensure a durable stickiness. If glued too soon or too late, quality is affected. Aiming big is not a bad thing either, but in our haste to accomplish so much, we can also miss out on important things that matter to us. Remaining small and capable is still a success if it means you can enjoy all the moving parts of your work without the unnecessary pressure.

> **Aiming big is not a bad thing either, but in our haste to accomplish so much, we can also miss out on important things that matter to us. Remaining small and capable is still a success if it means you can enjoy all the moving parts of your work without the unnecessary pressure.**

There is no need to pressure ourselves to move faster or be bigger than is appropriate. Rather, we should allot ourselves time to appreciate the process and time to recover from it. I think that each one of us has a definition of what a life well lived is and what constitutes a joyful and meaningful endeavor. It does not necessarily need to be big or fast. There is definitely beauty in being small and slow.

As a startup kid turned community maker, the power of small in the footwear industry became more relevant especially for advocating inclusivity in other creative industries. A common theme that we would repeat to ourselves is that "small together is big," connoting how scaling growth in the future economy shall be more mindful and inclusive from the ground up. We can enable small local communities and dynamic industries through helpful digital shift realities while also allowing them to remain authentic to their own selves, and through that value creation is allotted to many more. I believe that the coming together of the smaller units of the economy is a way for nation building towards a sustainable world.

Welcoming Diversity

Growing up, I would often hear about the successes of the men in our family, especially those who were prominent in the shoe business. In my process of getting to know our heritage more, I was able to learn that their accomplishments would not have been possible if it were not for the women in the family who were also successful entrepreneurs on their own accord. When the boys needed an extra hand in the business, they made ways to provide support both emotionally and financially, and they did so while taking care of their homes and families.

My parents raised me to challenge social norms by being a woman in professions that were often recognized to be in a "man's world." Whether it was in tech or in creative industries, being a female leader comes with an added challenge, but as we become more progressive, these fields are gradually becoming safe spaces for people of all genders. Half a century ago, the Philippine shoe industry was a male-dominated industry. Today, it is one of the most inclusive, with women taking the helm of the majority of enterprises. Here, there is neither age, race, nor any genders; only experience. All lines are blurred because the value that people uphold is how they are going to learn from each other. It is through this culture that more people are empowered to create freely, and everyone is celebrated for their contribution.

Valuing Different Perspectives

The greatest driver of change is to see the various ways you can approach a problem. When I founded Zapateria, the biggest challenge for the local shoe industry was the declining human capital. People were just not as interested in making shoes anymore. In terms of profession, many individuals opted not to pursue a career in artisan work. The common connotation was that there was no future in it, and because of that, the industry was in dire need of new talents. Much like my personal dilemma, the heritage of our craft needed to secure hope for a brighter tomorrow in order to survive and thrive. New talent was not the only thing we lacked though. We needed to develop a new mindset.

The way we make shoes is a multidisciplinary practice, converging art and science. The humanity behind footwear is the collaboration of people. Making a pair of shoes is driven by an ecosystem of expertise and practice. We learned that when people put their minds together, the most beautiful and most effective creations are made. Shoes become more personal.

In Zapateria, we have been able to work with practitioners from various backgrounds such as industrial design, fine arts, architecture, marketing, medicine, even economics and human resources. All their unique perspectives contributed to making our portfolio of amazing footwear and more importantly shaping our culture from the rigidity of an old school industry to a startup environment.

We have seen how our craft-based community has nurtured new and budding creatives, entrepreneurs, and innovators, even those who did not expect that they would be part of the footwear industry. From professional designers finding a new purpose, young students exploring a new passion, corporate executives willing to have a new sense of adventure, Zapateria became a space where they can be at their best, honing their skills and talents, being able to widen their network, and making a sustainable living out of what they create.

Seeing the potential of this new way of working with the community sparked a movement. We were eager to start the conversation not only among those in the same industry but also allied practitioners so that more people can advocate and contribute to the progression of the craft. Since we started Zapateria in 2017, organizations and government institutions have followed suit to our agenda. Today, there are academic programs dedicated to footwear development and entrepreneurship at schools in Marikina City as well as vocational courses for aspiring shoemakers. There are also government policies being lobbied to ensure trade and economic protection for footwear enterprises. All these efforts are coming to positive fruition to further encourage the next generation to celebrate and practice the craft that is worthy of having a place in the future.

Shaping a Collaborative Culture

They say "you cannot teach an old dog new tricks." In our experience, continuous learning can be enjoyable when you are with the right company. Zapateria started out by building a community that shares the same values and ideals for the future of footwear. This includes the veteran artisans who are dedicated to their craft mixed with the aspiring creatives who wish to learn more about its possibilities. With people also come different personalities and different experiences. Sometimes they clash and sometimes they jive, but when people work together, we are introduced to new ways of making things happen.

In Zapateria, we try our best not to turn down a design challenge as we believe through it we can improve. It is important to note that our team mostly consists of makers with decades of experience under their belt. Some of them are already past the age of retirement but are still working in the industry solely because of their passion for the craft. What amazes us the most is their willingness to take on new challenges. This is well complemented by the out-of-the-box ideas of our young collaborators who aspire to learn from them. The matchmaking between the two generations widens the possibilities for our shared craft, allowing each of them to learn deeply from each other, from producing eccentric designs to developing innovative ways of making or ways of working together.

Shoemaking by hand is not just a traditional craft. It evolves just as much as the people making the shoes. As times change and lifestyles shift, the craft too can innovate itself to adapt. It is a matter of being open to learning continuously and pushing ourselves to experiment with what we can create. And what better way to do that than with our own two hands?

C. Scaling Handmade

Shoemaking unlocked my true potential as a self-confessed geek who learned how to really love shoes. As a whole, my professional journey encompasses technology, entrepreneurship, and design. From building software to making shoes, I have valued more the importance of not only logic formation but creativity as well. I learned that the craft is a great means to advance critical thinking, problem solving, and even innovation.

Taking a look at the history of craft trade, long before industrialization, most of the necessities that we have come to enjoy were once made at the humble abode of a talented maker. The hand-made creation process still bears an admirable element that provides a sense of uniqueness and charm to every product. With every fold and stitch come years if not decades of mastery and a whole lot of heart just to come up with something worthy to be proud of.

Tracing fundamentals in the world of craft in footwear design and development, I realized all the more the importance of awakening the maker in us in pursuit of innovation. Integrating the concepts of a maker mindset powers up our imagination and helps us build the idea using resources within our reach. Makers make dreams come to life. Same with innovation, it needs to get out there and continuously evolve or adapt.

Craft is an art that can empower and liberate as it allows people to explore their own capabilities. This upholds the concept that one can begin on their own, with their ideas and skills, and grow independently. In the ever changing times, technology has also been a great contributor to innovation. The movement towards going digital has grown rampant. This brings up the need for it to be accessible and inclusive to most in order to adapt.

I believe in craft and the power of our hand, and that technology is a tool we can maximize to further its relevance without losing our soul. I went from the fast-paced world of tech to the slow and steady world of footwear. Polar in nature but I always knew that there is a way to marry both.

Many people are scared that technology will someday replace traditional craft. We, on the other hand, see an opportunity to use these advancements to adapt to the times without losing our fundamental craft. We see the progress of technology as a means for us to enhance handmade footwear, making them work hand-in-hand to allow longevity of human creativity and provide seamless experience for the patrons.

Imagine having a proof of ownership and authenticity of handmade products with trackability back to its socially responsible maker and supplier via Non-Fungible Token in Web3. It could also be a Shoemaking-as-a-Service pooling all the home-based or independent makers together to take on customized designs to distribute production as they come in the cloud.

Even AI, if used ethically can scale preservation and conservation of one's knowledge so that more generations can learn it. For example, it could have preserved the techniques of my father as an artisan and designer. It would be a treasure to be passed on to our descendants. It is about cherishing our most precious memories of his work and talent for me.

As someone who grew up in both worlds and has learned from each, technology and craft should not be alienated from each other. Technology is still only a tool, but humans power it, working with our hands makes wonder. There is always room to adapt without letting go of our authentic selves, our innate human form.

D. Molding Oneself

Contrary to the objections of how some members of my family think that I have thrown away bigger opportunities out there, making shoes made me whole that no money can buy. In every step of making a pair and our mis-steps, I understood myself and the people around me deeply. I found peace and even more love for our country. On top of it all, I realized that our heritage is only an anchor of how we are adapting to the many possibilities ahead of us from one generation to another.

Leonardo da Vinci once said that "The human foot is a masterpiece of engineering and a work of art." Shoes nowadays seem easy to come by, but believe it or not, working with shoes might just be one of the most complex jobs there is. You are working with so many moving parts. As challenging as it may seem, it gets harder especially if there is a need to work on making sure the foot measurements are designed to go above and beyond trying to ensure the best fit while also making it aesthetically pleasing.

Feet come in different shapes and sizes, much like the people who bare them, and that does not mean we will be creating a pair that depict their feet as is. Rather, it means we will craft shoes that will make them feel good about themselves, shoes that have a bold fit and can embody the unique story of its wearer beautifully and comfortably. Similar to how we can express ourselves through shoes, we are also the designers of our future.

"Feet come in different shapes and sizes, much like the people who bare them, and that does not mean we will be creating a pair that depict their feet as is. Rather, it means we will craft shoes that will make them feel good about themselves, shoes that have a bold fit and can embody the unique story of its wearer beautifully and comfortably. Similar to how we can express ourselves through shoes, we are also the designers of our future.

Reflecting on my tenure in this industry, a lot has changed, myself included. We should embrace our evolutions together – learning, coping, and growing as we should. Perhaps, in our own ways, it is about shaping our own mold and fitting into our own pair just like how I did not have to fill the same old shoes of my family. I just had to make my own. I did not allow their legacies and trials to cast a shadow over me. Bringing in my own ideologies and experiences while co-creating with the different players in the ecosystem, we shine a light so that a heritage that was once forgotten can stand on its own as a legacy built to last from fifth generation to generations of firsts beyond the bloodline.

Unyx Sta. Ana

Technopreneur/Community Maker

Graduating with honors with a degree in Computer Science at De La Salle University - Manila, Unyx Sta. Ana has more than a decade of experience in leading technology-based enterprises. She has built successful startups and led executive roles in the digital transformation for Philippines' largest firms. Her first company in automated advertising compliance and media analytics was acquired in 2017.

From being a technopreneur, Unyx, on its 5th generation of their family heritage in shoemaking since 1887, founded Zapateria, the Philippines' first creative hub for footwear design and development with a mission to foster creativity and innovation from one generation of soulful making to another.

She is an awardee of Asia-Pacific Economic Cooperation (APEC) Young Women Innovators, and one of the British Council Creative Innovators Program fellows. She received her Master of Science in Innovation and Business degree with High Distinction from Asian Institute of Management. She also serves as an Entrepreneur-in-Residence and consulting partner for startups, impact-led venture studios, and innovation hubs.

LinkedIn: www.linkedin.com/in/unyx
Website: www.zapateriahub.com
Instagram: www.instagram.com/zapateriahub/

Stephanie Tumampos

Looking through Life in a Scientific Lens

While sitting on the chair in my home office staring at the screen on a blank document trying to come up with ideas on how to write this biography or sort of it, it dawned on me that it is impossible to compress my life in a mere (but thousands!) number of words.

As a scientist, I always get the impression that I could only write with scientific jargon and that this chapter could be geeky, hence boring. But I hope my story, or series of stories, can inspire you with how science has greatly inspired me to be better in my career and as a person. And I hope this inspires you as well, child of the universe.

Me, the Anomaly

"What do you want to be?" This is one of the questions I often got when I was still a young girl in my primary school days. At first, I told them I wanted to reach the stars. A few months later, I changed my mind and told people who'd ask me the same question that I'd like to be a doctor.

Then, in my elementary days, I learned more careers that I could possibly take, and again, I changed my mind. This time, I wanted to be a diplomat.

It's fun to recall those younger days when dreaming was such a pleasure. It was like role play. Whenever I learned another career that seemed cool for me, I would immediately replace my career with another. But reality bit. Life was very hard. However, just like any Filipino family, everybody chipped in to give me a good education.

They say it takes a village to raise a kid. And this is what happened to me. My primary and elementary education was a product of the blood, sweat, and tears of the people who raised me, aside from my parents. These included my aunt, uncles, and grandmother. In high school, I went to a public science high school which didn't require tuition fees to be paid.

Although my family was willing to bet so much of their income for my education, I knew as the eldest in my family, there were more mouths to feed at home. My brother and sisters, too, needed a chance to also have a good education. My mind was already fixed on studying college in my island or in Cebu in whatever course that could possibly land me a job in the future, for me to freely choose where I could study or what I could study.

So in 2005, when applications for the country's state university opened, I could vividly remember how everyone was carefully choosing their courses and the campuses they wanted to stay in while I was at a corner, whisking my hand on the strings of the guitar trying to learn how to play it. I didn't put much thought on what course I would take. I just randomly selected the course which they said was one of the hardest courses – Applied Physics. I also chose the campus in Los Banos because I thought I just didn't like the idea of living in a big city.

Months passed. I took the exam, and suddenly, it was already time to know who passed the entrance exams when the university released the results online. And voila, my name was there. PASSED.

Stephanie Tumampos | BS Applied Physics
Los Baños Campus

There was definitely a mix of emotions, but what obviously surfaced was fear. Not because I was afraid to study one of the hardest courses offered in the university, but I feared I wouldn't be able to study in this prestigious university. This was because a part of me wanted to know if I could make it.

Back in the 2000-2010 decade, Filipino nurses were one of the most in-demand careers abroad, most especially in the United States. In my dad's view, it was a career that would give us a chance at a better and comfortable life. So when he learned that I wanted to pursue studies with the course he thought would not take me through life, he tried every ounce of his might to discourage me from sending my "yes" response to enroll in a university far from home.

"What kind of job will you get if you graduate from applied physics?" This was his question. Of course, my young mind didn't know anything. He answered with, "You'll only be a teacher."

I don't blame my dad, and for my readers, please don't blame your parents if they think otherwise of your decisions. I understand that my dad's words came from a place of love, and he worried that I might not be financially sustainable in the future. Our parents act this way because they only want what's best for us. I blame the society and the government, who for so long has given teachers so much work but with little pay, covering their hard work and effort with only flowery words.

Back to my story. So I told my dad, "What's wrong with being a teacher?" My dad wanted me to be a nurse and because everyone around him, such as his friends, had kids who were also planning to take up nursing as a degree. I guess everyone back then was taking up this course, and it's valid because in a study published by Yasmin Ortiga in 2018 in The Russell Sage Foundation Journal of the Social Sciences[1], there was just an increase of Filipino nurses overseas from 2010-2015 with slight decreases in between the first ten years due to world economic struggles.

---

[1] Ortiga, Yasmin. (2018). Learning to Fill the Labor Niche: Filipino Nursing Graduates and the Risk of the Migration Trap. RSF: The Russell Sage Foundation Journal of the Social Sciences. 4. 172. 10.7758/rsf.2018.4.1.10.

Just to clear the air, there is no problem in taking up nursing. I think it's a very good degree that could land me a good job and a possible ticket to greener pastures. I admire nurses for their dedication to work because this job is about saving lives. The problem with me being a nurse is I have heavy hands. I don't think I can gently push a needle into a patient's vein, nor do I have the qualities of being a nurse.

My dad and I had to argue about this for days. My mom, however, was supportive. To cut the long story short, I won this debate. And the rest is history. I completed my degree in Applied Physics, took a master's degree in Environmental Engineering at another campus, took another master's degree in GeoData Science abroad through a scholarship (double master's degree which technically gives me a total of three master's degrees), and I am currently working on my doctoral degree in Germany, also under a scholarship.

In retrospect with the title of this subsection, I call myself the anomaly. I did not choose what was normal or what was expected of me. I did not go with the flow. By definition according to Merriam-Webster, anomaly is a deviation from the common rule or the standard. This holds a tiny negative connotation in society. In science, an anomaly is also similarly defined as something that doesn't fit within a pattern. But science has a funny relationship with its definition because in our field, we don't treat anomalies as a faulty interpretation or systematic failure. Anomalies are also precursors to great discoveries and advances in science that we could never imagine.

Be who you need to be despite the loud noises around you and the demands of the world.

“Be who you need to be despite the loud noises around you and the demands of the world.

Survivorship Bias and the Significance of Insignificance

This won't come as a shock to anyone who knows me, but for almost a decade, I have received rejection after rejection in my applications for a scholarship to study abroad. My family and closest friends know how much I invested in writing personal essays, rearranging the format of my resume, and asking former mentors and professors to provide recommendation letters sealed in an envelope addressed to the university I applied to. Yet, year after year, I have only been at the short end of the stick, always on the shortlist and never making the cut.

You see, it has always been my dream to study in a prestigious university abroad. I guess I truly believed in the old adage, "Education is the key to success in life." But for the longest time, my dreams have made me feel small and inadequate. At certain times, I would feel that I don't measure up, that I am less of who I am and what I know, and that nothing was significant in me that would make those people behind the admissions portal choose me for the scholarship and an opportunity to study in their university.

However within that near-decade-long rollercoaster of emotions and rejections, it humbled me. It made me realize that there is so much that I needed to improve within myself, and that includes being graceful in defeat, learning that patience is a superpower, and that delays are a gift.

Looking back, I finally appreciated why I had to be rejected. And within those years of rejection, I pushed myself to discover new things.

I became a photographer and a writer for a national newspaper. I went on to do outreach activities in astronomy and space science, teaching less fortunate kids about the wonders of the Earth and the universe and also designing an educational curriculum for this subject. I also managed to assist my supervisor in the National Space Development Program which led to the establishment of the Philippine Space Agency.

For many, it was an unconventional way of dealing with the situation I was in. Others have told me I should have focused on getting a high-paying job, while others have said I was a failure in life.

"What's a graduate of applied physics doing in the media and journalism world?" whispered the naysayer, while another said, "Maybe she's a failure in the scientific field." I would be lying to say it didn't hurt. It did, but I knew that I had to trust the process.

The reason why I'm sharing my failures and setbacks is because I want people to see that my success is composed of ninety percent failures and the rest is luck.

Guess what? Today, I'm living the dream. I am back on track doing exactly what I love: science research and science communication. Yet, I fully know that many of those who never knew my journey might think that my success is linear, overlooking the fact that I had experienced failures, heartbreaks, and setbacks.

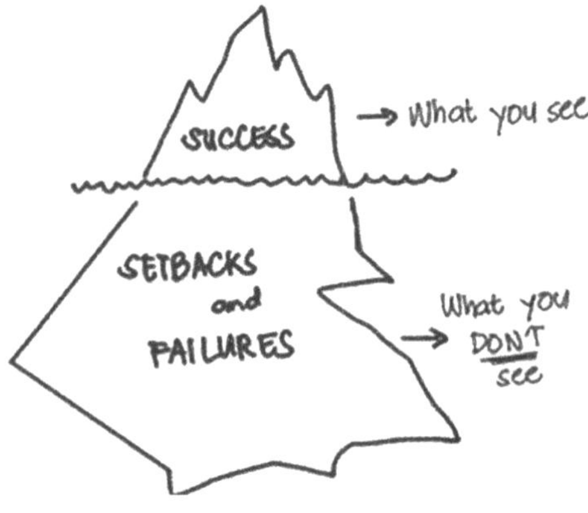

In science, we have a term called survivorship bias. Survivorship bias is when we only focus on the success subgroup while overlooking the failure subgroup, and assuming that the whole of the case is successful. It is extremely dangerous to think this way.

This is why in this chapter, I want you to understand that failures and setbacks are integral to your success. I'm emphasizing my failures because these are the foundation blocks that build the road to your ambitions and aspirations in life. These failures might seem insignificant, but they are the most significant in the process of success.

The Butterfly Effect of Paying it Forward

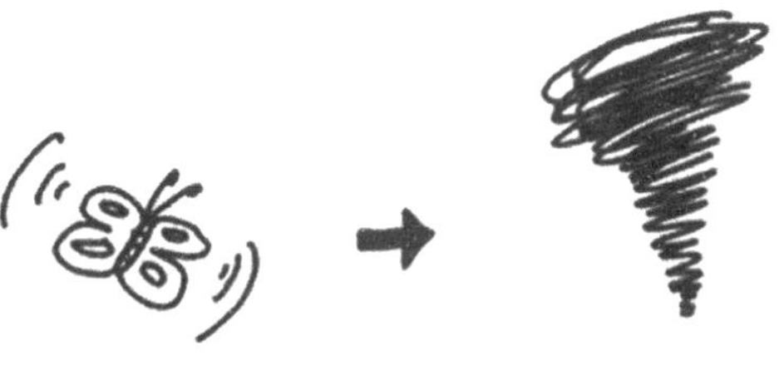

There are three questions I'd always ask people when I'm invited to speak or give lectures. And I'd like to ask these questions here too. The answers I require from these questions are people who are living today. So, are you ready? Here we go.

- Who is your favorite scientist?
- Who is your favorite scientist from your country?
- Who is your favorite female scientist from your country?

When I first thought of these questions, I had to ponder for a long time before I fully grasped that there is something wrong with how we inspire people to appreciate science. I realized that growing up, I didn't have any role models in science except of course Albert Einstein, Isaac Newton, and Marie Curie, to which all of them have already rested in power.

What's more baffling is that I could not identify someone from my country, more so a female scientist, who I could have looked up to while growing up. It's such a sad case for representation. How could young Filipinos appreciate science if they don't have someone to look up to?

I'm not here to promote science to inspire Filipinos to become scientists in the future. But, if they could look up to someone they can identify with, then maybe they'd start to explore the amazing wonders of science and how its technological advances and products are positively affecting our day-to-day activities like the mobile phone and the wireless transmission technology that helps us connect with each other from anywhere around the world.

So how do we do this? Should we ramp up our education system to promote science in every way possible? Actually, yes and no. Yes, because we need to constantly check our curriculum and evaluate its learning effectiveness to students. And no, because if it takes years for curriculum evaluations to happen, my fellow scientists, especially women, I'd like to invite you to step up and use our communication skills to introduce the wonders of our research to the Filipinos, especially the younger generation.

We have to pass down our learnings, discoveries, and skills. And although you might think that this can only have a small effect versus the millions of young Filipinos that need to be inspired, think about the butterfly effect. The butterfly effect, in scientific definition, is an idea where one small occurrence can influence a larger, complex system – that one small flap of the butterfly's wings can create a cyclone.

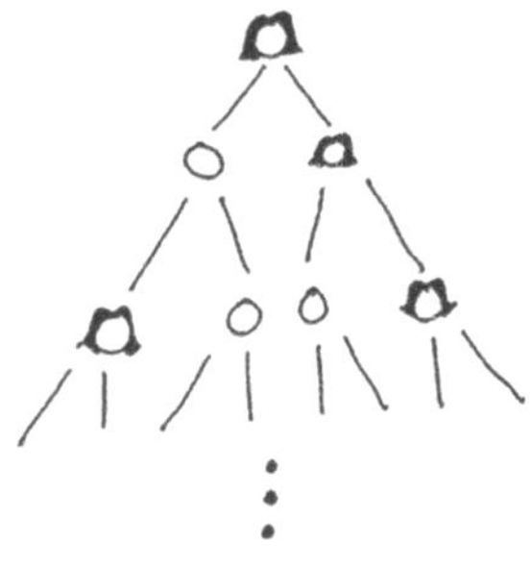

And why do we need to do this? Why do we need to inspire young Filipinos? So they may become scientists and help solve the country's problems through our science? Actually, no. We need to inspire children to be interested in science because in this subject, we introduce the scientific method. The scientific method is a process where we observe or think of a problem, create hypotheses, gather and explore the data and test an experiment, analyze results, gather conclusions, and make recommendations.

What's so important with the scientific method? If we teach and inspire the younger generation to practice the scientific method, we train to become better decision-makers and critical thinkers. They would not fall for any propaganda and false information because they know how to scrutinize any situation. It will become a habit, and in everyday life, they can make better choices. And when they're qualified to, choose the right leaders in their time.

Steph, Let's Skip the Science for Now

Vitruvian self-portrait

Alright, I hear you. I'm trying to relay scientific humor in each chapter, but it could be too much for some. So let's leave the science for now.

So, here we are. As I've said, I'm living the dream, and there's no other way than up, right? But what's next? What is my next dream? I can actually think a lot! And maybe I can even achieve them! Or not! I think I still have a lot of years that I could use to pursue good careers after I obtain my doctoral degree. I could be a professor back at home, or I could work in a big company. These lofty dreams make me excited. I can have excellent versions of myself.

But who will I be when I'm 60 or 70 years old? When I start to think about this, I can't help but wonder who Stephanie will be thirty or forty years from now.

One time, on a cold, drizzling night in Munich, I suddenly decided to pick up a package at one of the pack stations near my home. While waiting for the tram, an old lady came to me and asked in Deutsch,

"Wissen Sie, wann die Straßenbahn kommt?" In English, this would mean, "Do you know when the tram is coming?"

Despite my limited Deutsch skills, I still managed to reply that the tram would arrive in ten minutes.

"Ah! In zehn Minuten!" I said and added, "Ich spreche nicht sehr gut Deutsch. Das tut mir sehr leid." The last sentence meant that I didn't speak Deutsch well and that I was sorry.

She immediately switched to speaking English, and that was how we started our short conversation.

"Where do you come from?" she asked. And of course I said, "I'm from the Philippines" to which she replied, "That is so far from here." I smiled and told her that I'm only here to study and obtain my doctoral degree.

The Philippines reminded her of the warm weather, and she shared that she has been to warmer countries before. She then shifted our conversation to traveling.

"I miss traveling, especially in warmer countries. Germany is too cold," she said. I nodded my head and agreed. She continued.

"Twenty years ago, when I was around sixty years old and got separated from my husband, I went on a backpacking trip for 10 years in South America. I noticed that people living in warmer climates are also warm and welcoming. I traveled around Mexico, Brazil, and Peru, and I never felt I was in danger. When I needed cash, I worked part-time taking care of old people there like me."

The tram arrived and we both boarded. She spoke again while I was pleasantly listening to her story.

"Maybe it's the weather here in Germany. This is why I enjoy taking saunas every week to warm myself up. I'm now 82 years old. I don't have much, but I'm content with my life and how it turned out," while she chuckled with her eyes glistening under those red-framed, cat-eye shaped glasses.

I was two more stops away, and I had to alight on my station. I didn't miss the opportunity to tell her that she made me feel hopeful with life when I reach her age and when things don't go as I imagine it to be simply because this is how life is. It is full of ironies.

The moral of this story is not scientific, but I would like to share this to you readers. I want you to realize that when life makes us feel small, I hope that we will have the courage to turn things around. And that our insignificance should lift us to make it significant. That when we're old and wrinkly and life hammers us down, we would still be able to find ourselves curious and ever exploring the world, while living in contentment with what life could offer.

"

I want you to realize that when life makes us feel small, I hope that we will have the courage to turn things around. And that our insignificance should lift us to make it significant. That when we're old and wrinkly and life hammers us down, we would still be able to find ourselves curious and ever exploring the world, while living in contentment with what life could offer.

We Are All Made Up of Stardust

We're back in science, and we're going to talk about YOU, the star.

Perhaps the most significant gift science has ever given mankind is the discovery that we are all made up of, in fact, stardust. It sounds a bit surreal, but in a research led by female astrophysicist Eleanor Margaret Burbidge in 1957, she and her team extracted the composition of stars and published their findings in a paper entitled, "Synthesis of the Elements in Stars."[2]

Through this research, we found out that nearly all the elements that are intertwined in our DNA to the atoms inside our body – oxygen, hydrogen, carbon, nitrogen, calcium, phosphorus, potassium, sulphur, sodium, chlorine, magnesium, to name a few – were all made from stars.

The building blocks of the universe, from all the living and non-living things on Earth to the planets and the rest of the celestial bodies found in outer space, come from cosmic processes of bursting supernovas scattering elements as products in vast cosmic space creating new star systems. And that star system is also YOU.

So on days when everything feels impossible, look into yourself because there's a universe within you, and inside that is a galaxy with endless possibilities.

---

[2] Burbidge, E. M., Burbidge, G. R., Fowler, W. A., & Hoyle, F. (1957). Synthesis of the Elements in Stars. Rev. Mod. Phys., 29, 547–650. doi:10.1103/RevModPhys.29.547

Stephanie Tumampos

Stephanie Tumampos is a Filipino doctoral student at the Technical University of Munich, Germany, in the field of remote sensing. She has a background in applied physics, environmental engineering, and geoinformatics. Stephanie has always been fascinated about how the Earth works and how present technologies can give a digital representation of our planet so we may be able to address some of the problems we face, including climate change.

Aside from her academic pursuits, Stephanie is also a passionate science communicator where she was a photojournalist and science writer for BusinessMirror for seven years before moving to Europe to pursue her academic career. She currently hosts the podcast, "Down to Earth: A Podcast for Geoscientists by Geoscientist," of the IEEE Geoscience and Remote Sensing Society (IEEE GRSS) where she invites experts in the field of innovative geoscience and remote sensing to talk about their science, careers, and passions. As such, she is also an advocate for diversity, inclusion, and belongingness. Stephanie believes that every person should be able to do science regardless of gender, race, or background. She also believes that science should be accessible to all.

She promotes all of these through the IEEE GRSS, which she serves as the Chief of Publicity and PR, social media ambassador for IEEE GRSS Inspire Develop Empower Advance (IDEA) committee, and International Society for Digital Earth where she is currently the Youth Ambassador, among others. In her free time, and when she's in the Philippines, she loves to free dive in the waters of her home island, Bohol.

Sharon Vaswani

The Lotus Effect: Blossoming of a Leader

The Roots – The Foundation of a Leader

Every morning as I wake up with the rising sun filtering through my bedroom window, a Hindu prayer, the *Hanuman Chalisa,* taught to me in childhood by my mother, comes to my lips. This prayer invoking the Lord to purify my mind and invoke strength to face the joys and challenges of the day has been my comfort, guide, and anchor in my life.

For as long as I can remember, this ritual has been a way of connecting with something greater than myself. It has instilled in me a deep sense of values that I would say have been the formation of my leadership, guiding my decisions and shaping my character. Together with the values of empathy, compassion, and selflessness, which are very intrinsic to my belief system, these have taught me to always see beyond myself and to always strive for the greater good of all.

Having been brought up as a practicing Hindu in the predominantly Catholic country, Philippines, as I went to a Catholic elementary school and graduated from a Jesuit university, I have always stood out with my unique physical features. These differences, whether it was my deep-set eyes or the bridge of my nose, actually helped me cultivate more self-awareness and a deeper understanding of my own strengths and weaknesses. Rather than being a victim of prejudice, I found that adapting was a way for me to break barriers and build bridges. I feel I embody the billboard that says "FIT IN, STAND OUT." Living in this interfaith context was a sense of completion rather than competition for me. After all, diversity of thought makes us stronger, not weaker. The theory of evolution itself shows us that without diversity and adapting to changes in the environment, we die off as species.

In my scholastic days, I had always been interested in participating and taking an active role in various organizations, and the pinnacle of this for me was my tenure as President of the Student Council in my University. This was a very humbling experience for me, which taught me quite a few things. There really is no secret to being a successful leader. Getting things done was the result of preparation, hard work, and teamwork. Elevated standards created elevated results. These standards apply to not only what opportunities one works on, but also to the quality of work that one can expect from others in the team. If we say yes to mediocrity, then we will not have time for exceptional ones, and thus our growth can get hampered. As John Maxwell aptly put it, "You don't go into an opportunity; you grow into one."

Just as the fibrous roots of the lotus plant hold the plant to float in water, a strong foundation is also necessary to hold up and give strength to a leader. Without the unique contributions of individuals from various walks of life, the structure of leadership is weak and incomplete, much like a lotus without its roots. Embracing diversity not only strengthens the foundation of leadership, but it also allows for a rich tapestry of perspectives and experiences to flourish, ultimately leading to more innovative and effective solutions. Culture and values also play a fundamental role in anchoring the leader, providing nourishment and stability necessary for growth.

The Stem – Navigating the Challenges of Leadership

Look at the world today, and we see shifting market trends, changing weather patterns, and varying health issues, among others concerns. Constant changes in our surroundings bring about challenges. For those filled with laziness, they would fear challenges and give up; for those filled with aggressiveness, they would fight challenges and just give in, but for those filled with a sense of calmness, facing challenges is an opportunity to give more. For me, this has meant cultivating a mindset of flexibility and resilience.

As fate would have it, the COVID-19 pandemic struck just as I assumed my role as VP for Healthcare and Advocacies at the Chamber. I can't help but marvel at how I navigated through the challenges. It was as if fate had conspired to test my leadership abilities to the fullest. The pandemic brought with it a plethora of difficulties and challenges.

Communication became a major hurdle as face-to-face meetings were no longer an option. Travel was restricted, making it impossible to send the children with biliary atresia to India for their life-saving liver operation. But I refused to let this setback dampen our spirits. Instead, I set out to make the most of the resources available to me, determined to fulfill the mandate handed to me and continue carrying out the projects of the chamber. And so, I turned to technology. Virtual meetings became the norm, and soon connections were seamless as they were being made across geographical areas and different time zones. Without the constraints of physical distance, we were able to collaborate with more doctors and healthcare practitioners from different parts of the globe, sharing ideas and strategies to help us navigate throughout the pandemic. Imagine the power of sending a Twitter message as it enabled 36 people to fly to India for their liver transplant. During this time, I was able to assist in collecting donations from the Indian community worth PhP 12 million to provide support to the frontline workers in the country. And in response to the call of our times, a vaccine program was also rolled out for 48 member companies and their staff in Metro Manila. The pandemic may have presented numerous challenges, but it also showed me that with determination, resilience, and adaptability, we can overcome any obstacle that comes our way.

Another lesson that I learned during this time is that not all progress is visible. I learned not to beat myself up when I didn't see immediate results. To put it simply, making one healthy meal won't transform your diet, but it's a step in the right direction towards a healthier lifestyle. Or one workout won't shed the inches on your waistline, but it may be better than no workout. The daily grind and consistently putting in the effort towards achieving tasks and objectives is crucial for successful leadership. Results are accumulated in drops, and one must be careful not to lose them in buckets.

Navigating the ever-changing landscape of leadership can be likened to the delicate stem of the lotus flower. Much like the stem that needs to withstand the wind and rain in order to reach its full potential, it is through challenges that one is able to learn and grow. Consistently putting in effort and being careful not to undo our progress are also crucial elements in this journey, for just as a strong gust of wind can uproot the fragile stem of the lotus, so too can a moment of carelessness undo all the progress we have made.

> **"Navigating the ever-changing landscape of leadership can be likened to the delicate stem of the lotus flower. Much like the stem that needs to withstand the wind and rain in order to reach its full potential, it is through challenges that one is able to learn and grow. Consistently putting in effort and being careful not to undo our progress are also crucial elements in this journey, for just as a strong gust of wind can uproot the fragile stem of the lotus, so too can a moment of carelessness undo all the progress we have made.**

The Leaves – Growing and Developing as a Leader

Continuous education is essential both personally and professionally as it keeps one updated with the latest developments in the industry, informed of emerging trends and equipped with the tools to achieve goals. They say that the capacity to learn is a gift; the ability to learn is a skill; and the willingness to learn is a choice. This has been a conscious undertaking on my part to seek out new opportunities for growth and challenge myself to learn new skills and approaches. The driving force behind my commitment to continuous learning and development is *ikigai*, a Japanese concept that translates to "a reason for being." As I look for the intersection of what I love, what I am good at, what the world needs, and what I can be paid for, it helps me gain insight into what I can contribute to a specific area in life. Whether it is through attending industry conferences or taking online courses, I am committed to staying up-to-date with the latest developments in my field. As an optometrist, pursuing Continuing Professional Development (CPD) courses not only helps me become accredited but also guides my choices in molding my company to provide the best possible eyecare services. Moreover, this commitment to mastery is a key component of my leadership approach that allows me to inspire and motivate my team to strive for excellence. Another concept that has been instrumental is that of *kaizen* which translates to "continuous improvement." With this philosophy that encourages individuals and organizations to constantly strive for excellence by making small, incremental improvements over time, I have been able to encourage my team to embrace *kaizen* and always look for ways to improve their skills and processes.

One's environment plays an essential role that can help make the desired behavior the default behavior. An example of this is by joining various groups, which is similar to joining a book club if you wanted to read more or joining a runner's club if you wanted to run more. As they say, the environment that you plant yourself in will do the heavy lifting for you if you align it to where you want to go.

As such, emanating from my business strategy, I actively involved myself with other organizations, including the Indian Women in Enterprise (I-WE), which emphasizes the importance of collaboration, communication, and having a shared responsibility. It is about creating an environment where everyone is empowered to contribute to the success of the team. The various initiatives of the organization create a supportive and dynamic culture that encourages everyone to reach their full potential.

My most recent and impactful contribution towards women empowerment was the Tech2Transform project under I-WE, which was aimed at addressing the fact that 38% of MSMEs in the country had to shut down due to COVID-19. Through the five-month-long digital series, participated by 27 women-led MSME (WMSME)s across eight verticals around the country, I helped to address gender inequalities in STEM and empowered women-led businesses to make use of tools in gathering data, marketing, and financing. I also had the opportunity to be a mentor and training partner for the Women Strong Network, a consortium of over 120 WMSEs. The successful first batch of Tech2Transform program has enabled the creation of an ecosystem of WMSME enablers, paving the way for the scalability and replicability of this endeavor in the coming years.

While there were certainly challenges along the way, I am grateful for the role I played in supporting WMSMEs and helping to create an ecosystem that will continue to drive their growth. The duration of the program alone had the impact of improving participants' profitability up to 64% and business expansion and scalability over 85%. Thus like the leaves of the lotus which provide sustenance to the plant, one's environment or the organizations that one is part of can help your growth and development as a leader. Also, the leaves of the lotus help to repel water and resist damage, which makes it a symbol for the transformative power of surroundings on growth.

Moreover, mentorship and coaching can have a tremendous impact on leadership success. Through the guidance and support of my mentors, I have been able to develop my own leadership skills and become a more effective communicator, collaborator, and problem solver. And so, as a leader, I am committed to paying it forward by participating in mentorship events of GoNegosyo to help other MSMEs unlock their full potential and achieve their own leadership goals. Leadership is about upscaling both present and future leaders.

The Flowers – Leadership with a Purpose

The lotus begins as a small bud, but with the help of sunlight, it breaks the surface of water and is unmarked by the dirt that surrounds it. It blooms into a stunning masterpiece. Similarly, a leader emerges out of one's vision and perseverance. Through my own journey, I've learned that leadership is not just about achieving personal success, but about uplifting those around you so that the decisions made with purpose at the heart have a positive and sustainable impact for all stakeholders.

Through my experiences in both my professional career and various engagements in social work as a leader, I have made it my mission to help uplift the status of my countrymen. It's not just about running successful companies, but about making a positive impact. I firmly believe that as leaders, we have a responsibility to promote responsible sourcing, employee welfare, and other non-discriminatory practices that meet fundamental responsibilities in the areas of human rights, labor, environment and anti-corruption. This is why I became a signatory of the Women's Empowerment Principles for both the surgical and pharmaceutical companies that I lead.

Leadership is not just about policies and practices. Rather it is about having a positive mindset and being willing to take calculated risks. Being focused on delivering quality medical supplies, I continually encourage my staff to strictly adhere to the standards set forth by governing institutional bodies. It is this attention to detail and commitment to excellence that has allowed me to carve out opportunities and help me make a real impact in my field. One example of this impact is the partnership between my company, PanOphthalmics, and Manila Central University's College of Optometry community extension program. By working together, we are able to amplify the impact of visual programs and promote eye and vision health awareness throughout the nation.

The Lotus – A Symbol of Leadership Excellence

Like a lotus that begins as a small bud and blooms into a beautiful flower, similarly with the power of setting a vision and clear goals, a leader blooms into a stunning masterpiece. It also is a constant reminder that even in the murkiest of waters, beauty can still thrive. As leaders, we must be willing to navigate the challenges and uncertainties of our environment, but with a clear vision and unwavering determination, we too can blossom into something truly remarkable.

> **Like a lotus that begins as a small bud and blooms into a beautiful flower, similarly with the power of setting a vision and clear goals, a leader blooms into a stunning masterpiece. It also is a constant reminder that even in the murkiest of waters, beauty can still thrive. As leaders, we must be willing to navigate the challenges and uncertainties of our environment, but with a clear vision and unwavering determination, we too can blossom into something truly remarkable.**

Through my own journey, I've learned that leadership is about being patient and trusting the process. One mustn't rush things or try to force growth, but instead have faith in one's team and allow things to happen naturally, like how a lotus flower trusts its own unfolding. A good leader should also be adaptable and able to pivot when necessary to steer their team towards success. Being open-minded and flexible helps to overcome unexpected challenges.

It's not just about achieving personal success, but also about uplifting those around you. It's about recognizing the potential in others and guiding them towards achieving their goals. Just as the lotus flower pods contain seeds that can grow into new plants, a good leader should likewise plant the seeds of change and growth in their team, encouraging them to learn new skills, take on new challenges, and push themselves to be even better. By understanding and supporting their team members, leaders can create a positive and inclusive work environment where everyone feels valued and supported.

You define work by what you get; but you define life by what you give. The lotus flower releases a sweet scent to attract insects for pollination. A good leader should also attract and inspire their team to achieve their goals and reach their full potential. A leader too must have a sense of purpose and connection to the team, their organization, and their community.

As I reflect on my experiences as a leader, I cannot help but draw parallels between the development of a lotus flower and effective leadership. The lotus flower, with its ability to repel water droplets and stay pristine even in muddy conditions, provides a powerful metaphor for resilience and adaptability. Adopting the lotus effect in my leadership style has allowed me to blossom into a strong, effective, and impactful leader.

Sharon Vaswani

Dr. Sharon is the Founder and CEO of PanOphthalmics, a platform for sourcing surgical instruments, and is also the Chairwoman of Fortis Medi Pharmaceutical, Inc. – a pharmaceutical manufacturing plant. Sharon has been acclaimed as part of the 2022 Circle of Excellence in Young Entrepreneur and Young SHERO of the year award categories of the Asia CEO Awards.

In line with her goal of wanting to make effective contributions to society, she served as VP at the Federation of Indian Chamber of Commerce Philippines, where despite travel restrictions, she continued the life-saving project for children with biliary atresia, aided in assembling a donation worth PhP 12 million from the Indian community, and helped to conduct a vaccine roll-out program. Currently, she is a co-founder and the Vice President of Indian Women in Enterprise where she was instrumental in Tech2Transform, a five-month program that digitally trained 27 women-led MSMEs across eight verticals towards growth.

From a young age, she has also been involved with people from different regions and backgrounds as an active Global Interfaith leader affiliated with the United Religions Initiative and Rotary International. Just recently, she was also conferred as the 2022 Champion for Youth Leadership by UN Women.

https://www.linkedin.com/in/sharonvaswani